INTROD

Psychology

Nigel C. Benson

Edited by Richard Appignanesi

ICON BOOKS UK   TOTEM BOOKS USA

This edition published in the UK
in 1999 by Icon Books Ltd.,
Grange Road, Duxford,
Cambridge CB2 4QF
email: icon@mistral.co.uk
www.iconbooks.co.uk

Distributed in the UK, Europe,
Canada, South Africa and Asia by the
Penguin Group: Penguin Books Ltd.,
27 Wrights Lane, London W8 5TZ

This edition published in Australia
in 1999 by Allen & Unwin Pty. Ltd.,
PO Box 8500, 9 Atchison Street,
St. Leonards NSW 2065

Previously published in the UK and
Australia in 1998 under the title
Psychology for Beginners

Reprinted 1998, 1999

First published in the United States
in 1999 by Totem Books
Inquiries to: PO Box 223,
Canal Street Station,
New York, NY 10013

In the United States,
distributed to the trade by
National Book Network Inc.,
4720 Boston Way, Lanham,
Maryland 20706

Library of Congress Catalog
Card Number: 98–060267

Originating editor: Richard Appignanesi

Printed and bound in Australia
by McPherson's Printing Group, Victoria

WHAT IS PSYCHOLOGY?

"Psychology" comes from two words: **psyche** and **logos**. The word psyche (pronounced "sigh-key") is from the Greek word ψυχη – meaning "breath of life", i.e. "soul or spirit", loosely translated as MIND.

And logos means "knowledge", "study": like all "ologies"!
In Greek mythology, Psyche was represented by a butterfly. She became the wife of Eros, the god of love (renamed Cupid by the Romans).

The Greek letter Ψ (spelled "psi", and pronounced "sigh") is now used as the international symbol for Psychology.

Hence, Psychology was originally defined as: **the study of the mind.**

But, this isn't how most Psychologists define Psychology today.

Towards a Definition

Most Psychologists try hard to make a clear distinction between what *is* proper Psychology, and what *isn't*.

So, how do Psychologists define "Psychology"? Well, there are difficulties in finding one universally accepted definition. Although most Psychologists agree that it is important to be *scientific* – to avoid muddled thinking – it's not always clear exactly what this means.

Another difficulty is the practical problem – some say "impossibility"! – of studying the "mind" directly. Indeed, even trying to define "mind" is very difficult. Some Psychologists have avoided this completely, especially the Behaviourists, like B. F. Skinner and J. B. Watson.

"We do not need to try to discover what personalities, states of mind, feelings... really are in order to get on with a scientific analysis of behaviour."
Skinner (1971)
"Never use the terms *consciousness, mental states, mind...*"
Watson (1913)

In practice, therefore, most Psychologists concentrate on what is **observable** and **measurable** in a person's behaviour, including the biological processes in the body. At the same time, despite the extreme views of certain Behaviourists, the "mind" is still generally considered to be central to the subject.

Thus, a commonly accepted "working definition" is:

Psychology is the scientific study of the mind and behaviour of humans and animals.

Doesn't that definition also apply to Sociology?
It is similar, but Sociology is generally about the study of *large groups* of people – in *societies* or *sub-cultures.*

Psychology, on the other hand, is mainly about individuals or small groups of people, as in Social Psychology.

There are also differences in the *methods* used. In Psychology, there is emphasis on *experiments,* but in Sociology that method is not usually possible – for practical and ethical reasons – so *observations* and *surveys* are more commonly used.

What Does Psychology Include?

Unlike the Natural Sciences, Psychology doesn't have one unifying theory or particular approach...

We shall look at the 6 main approaches or perspectives within Psychology:

PSYCHODYNAMIC; BEHAVIOURISM; COGNITIVE (including Gestalt); HUMANISTIC; BIO-PSYCHOLOGICAL; SOCIAL-CULTURAL

The Sections Within Psychology

In addition to the different perspectives, the subject can be divided into various areas of study in university departments. A typical division would look like this:

To qualify as a Psychologist requires a recognized qualification at degree level (e.g. BSc Hons) and membership of a relevant Professional Association, for example one of the following:
the BPS – British Psychological Society (founded 1901),
the APA – American Psychological Association (founded 1893),
the APS – American Psychological Society (founded 1988).

Psychology and Psychiatry?

There is a common confusion between the two. Put simply, the difference is this:

Psychiatrists have a Medical Degree, plus a Psychiatric Qualification, and belong to a Medical Association. (Only they have the authority to prescribe drugs.) But some Psychologists also specialize, with extra training, in helping people with mental disorders – they are Clinical Psychologists.

To qualify as a Clinical Psychologist requires a good Psychology Degree (at least a 2.1) plus relevant work experience (e.g. nursing, social or care work) and a recognized Clinical qualification (e.g. a BPS approved Diploma or Masters Degree).

Some Clinical Psychologists base their therapies, like traditional Psychiatrists, on *Psychoanalysis* (e.g. the Tavistock Clinic), while others use *Behaviour Therapy and Modification* (e.g. the Maudsley Clinic). (These therapies are described later.)

Is Psychology a Science?

Since the definition includes "scientific study", this begs the question: "What is Science?". To most people, "science" conjures up images of laboratories with test-tubes, complex measuring equipment, etc. This is appropriate because it emphasizes the importance of EXPERIMENTS, which can only be properly carried out in controlled conditions.

Experiments are conducted to try to find the CAUSES of EFFECTS, in all scientific subjects.

So, Psychologists have to use various research METHODS other than just experiments.

METHODOLOGY

The study of methods of research is called "methodology". There are two aspects to this:
(a) the more PRACTICAL considerations about which research methods should be used, and
(b) the more PHILOSOPHICAL questions about the nature of SCIENCE itself. Let's start with practical methodology.

Within each method, various TECHNIQUES can be used, e.g. audio and/or video recording, questionnaires, interviews, tests, measurements, etc.

Research Methods: 1 Experiment

The first Social Psychology experiment was by Triplett (1898) who tested the hypothesis (prediction) that boys would wind fishing reels more quickly in pairs than alone.

Average times to complete 150 turns of a fishing reel, pulling toy horses:

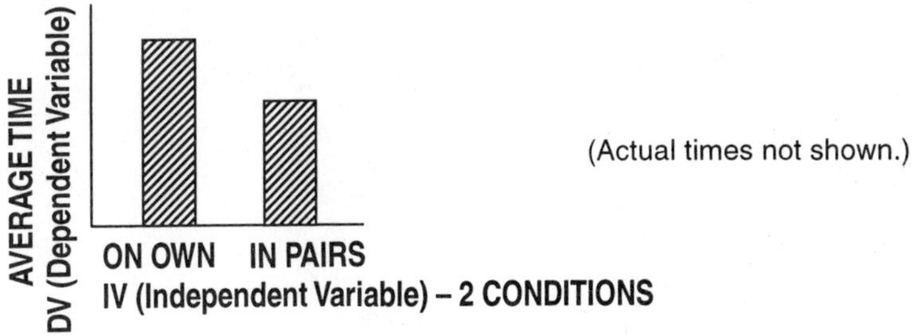

This has the characteristics of all experiments. One "cause" variable (IV) is changed and the "effect" (DV) is measured, while all other variables are CONTROLLED to remain the same. Two disadvantages are that they can be trivial and artificial.

2 Observation

A lot of information can be gained by observing behaviour, especially in more "natural" environments: home, school playgrounds, nursery. McIntyre (1972) observed children, aged 2-4 yrs, measuring aggression (according to predetermined ratings). Some of the results were:

Graph showing differences in aggression

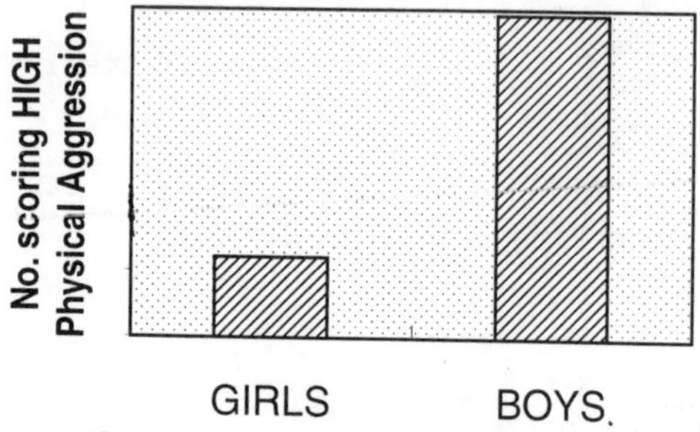

(Simplified data: actual measurements not shown.)

However, as this wasn't an experiment (no IV or "cause" variable), it's not possible to confidently say that gender is a "cause" of aggression. Also, there were many variables outside the researcher's control, e.g. parental discipline, books read, TV and films watched, etc.

3 Survey

This typically involves measuring **many** people, often using **questionnaires** and/or **interviews**, e.g. about attitudes. Wellings and others conducted the "National Survey of Sexual Attitudes and Lifestyles", published as *Sexual Behaviour in Britain* (1994).

One of the statements was: "Companionship and affection are more important than sex in a marriage or relationship."

Results:

	agree or strongly agree	*neither agree nor disagree*	*disagree or strongly/ disagree*	*sample size questioned*
men	**67.2%**	22.0%	10.8%	2079
women	**68.4%**	21.7%	9.9%	2563

Conclusion:

"Most noteworthy perhaps, given the emphasis placed on the importance of sex in some sections of the media (Brunt, 1982), is the sizable majority of respondents who do not see sex as the most important part of a marriage or relationship."

Two problems with surveys, indeed ALL research: are they RELIABLE, i.e. consistent, and VALID, i.e. accurate?

4 Case Study (or Case History)

This is a highly detailed account of an individual (or small group, e.g. a family). Oliver Sacks (1970) published the "Dr. P." case, about a cultured and popular musician. Tragically, he could no longer recognize people or objects, due to adulthood brain damage.

"He reached out his hand and took hold of his wife's head, tried to lift it off, to put it on. He had apparently mistaken his wife for a hat!"

Such neurological case studies can reveal a great deal about the brain. In this case, how certain parts control visualization, recognition and remembering. Thus, case (or "clinical") studies are very useful in Cognitive Psychology. They're also the foundation of Psychoanalysis.

5 Correlation

This is a measurement of the relationship between two (or more) variables. There are three types: Positive, None (Zero), and Negative. They can be shown as **scattergrams**.

Positive Correlation means: as one variable increases, so does the other. For example, when identical twins are measured for intelligence.

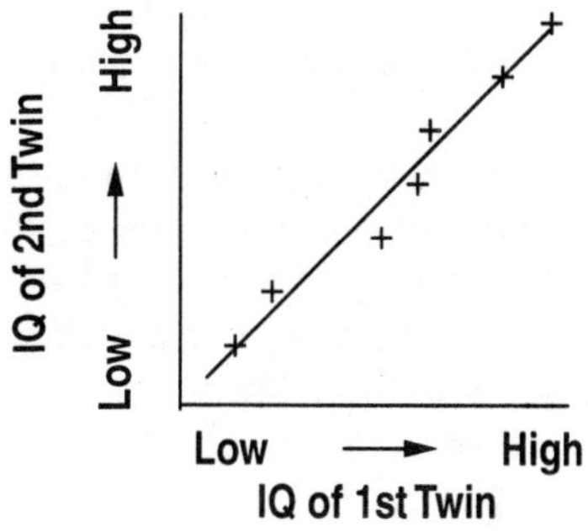

Non-correlation means: there is no relationship either positive or negative, e.g. between freckles and intelligence.

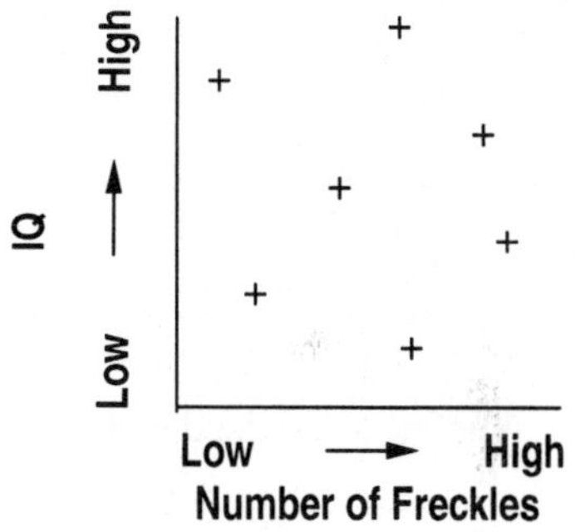

Negative Correlation means: as one variable increases, the other decreases, e.g. the older the man, the less hairs on the head.

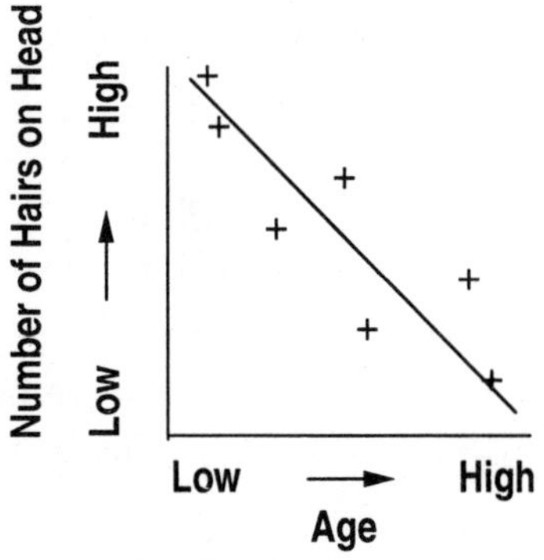

Correlation Scale and Significance

Correlation can also be shown as a number on a scale...

-1.0	.9	.8	.7	.6	.5	.4	.3	.2	.1	0	.1	.2	.3	.4	.5	.6	.7	.8	.9	1.0+

As a rule of thumb, about 0.6 or 0.7 or higher (+ or -) is usually significant. (Tables provide the exact figure for each sample size.)

But the most important thing to remember is that **correlation does not show causation.** A serious example of this common misunderstanding occurred in Italy. In the early 1980s, there were unexplained deaths where high mortality correlated positively with consumption of olive oil. The government leapt to the conclusion that the oil was poisonous. Later research showed it was tomatoes contaminated by pesticides that caused the deaths...

Basis of False Assumption

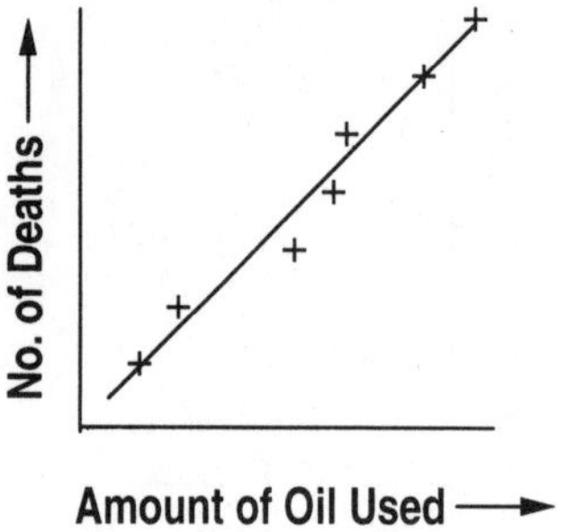

Actual Food Preparation

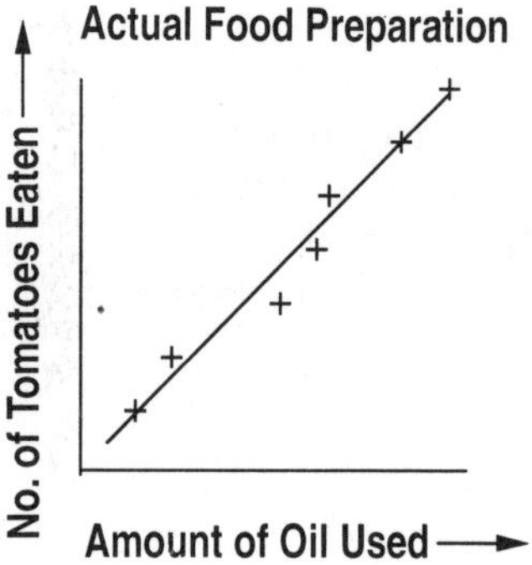

Actual Cause of Deaths

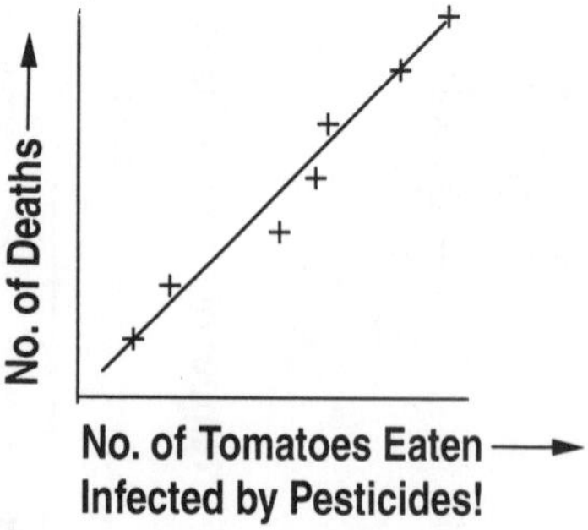

There's also the problem of SPURIOUS Correlations that occur by chance, e.g. increased alcohol sales and bicycles bought by priests.

Other Methodological Issues

In addition to deciding which method to use, Psychologists have to check that the **sample** selected is appropriate (in both quantity and quality), and that data collected is **reliable** and **valid**.

Sampling is the process of selecting a group of people – **participants** or, old term, "subjects" – for research. It's rarely possible to test the whole of the "population" under investigation, so a representative "sample" is used. There are 3 main ways of selecting:

Random sampling means that each person in the target "population" has an equal chance of being selected. This should provide typical participants.
For example, put the names in a hat, shuffle and then pick out 30.

Quota sampling uses certain numbers from specific groups, e.g. 20 from three different age groups. (This technique is also favoured by many "opinion poll" collectors, for example when surveying voters' intentions by selecting from a range of towns.)

Opportunistic sampling means "whoever is available at the time", which can of course produce biased results. (Most Psychological research uses university students!)

Reliability means being "repeatable" or "consistent". When a reliable test is used, it gives similar results in similar circumstances. (This can be tested by correlation, comparing the results of one study with another. Many tests are **standardized** in this way.)

However, just because a test or measurement is reliable doesn't mean it's valid.

Validity means the test or measurement used is actually measuring what's intended, e.g. that an IQ test measures "intelligence" (sometimes debatable!).

Philosophical Methodology

There is also a philosophical aspect to methodology. This asks fundamental questions. "How do we know whether something is true?"... "Is that theory correct?"... "Can we ever *prove* anything?"... "What is Science?"

For most people today, "science" is about taking MEASUREMENTS and coming up with THEORIES to explain things – with both processes working together. This approach may seem obvious, but it hasn't always been this way.

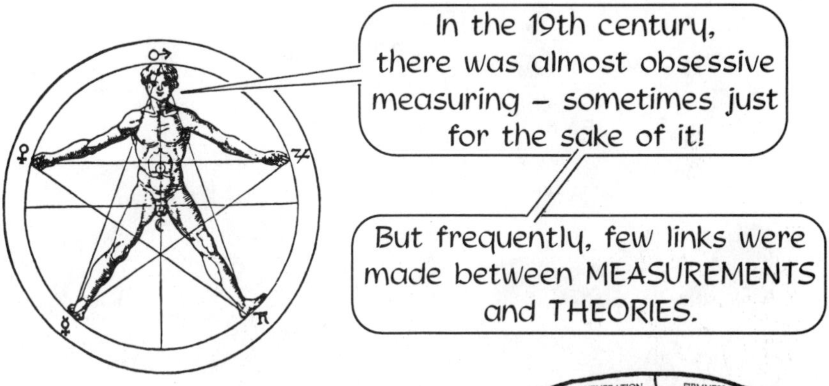

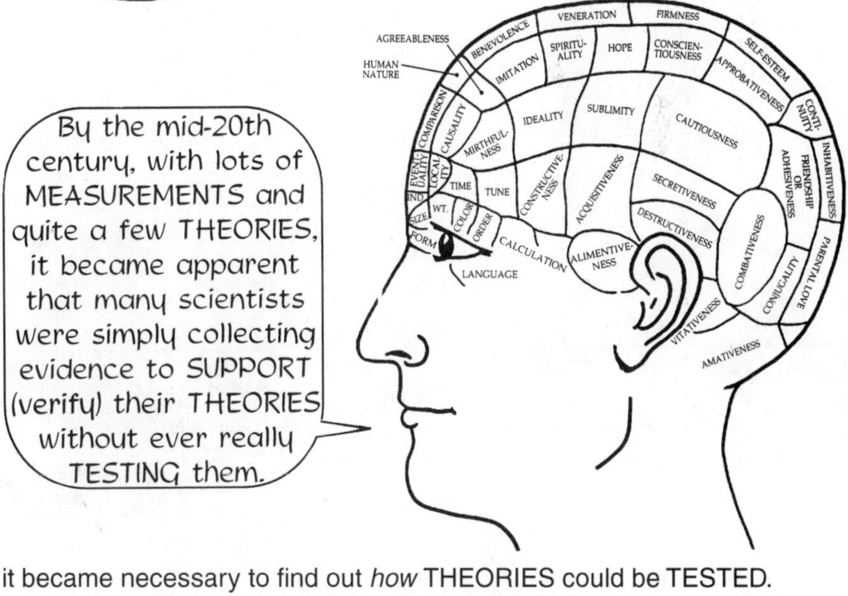

So it became necessary to find out *how* THEORIES could be TESTED. Indeed, just what *is* the difference between SCIENTIFIC and UNSCIENTIFIC THEORIES? One man provided a way to decide...

Karl Popper

Karl Popper (1902-94) set up a criterion: THEORIES can be divided into those that are SCIENTIFIC (i.e. disprovable) and those that are NON-SCIENTIFIC (i.e. not disprovable). NON-SCIENTIFIC THEORIES include: most religious ideas (e.g. The Existence of God), many political ideas (Marxism, Capitalism), Freudian ideas (e.g. the contents of the Unconscious Mind), and daily horoscopes found in newspapers.

Non-Scientific Theories have the appeal that they can explain EVERYTHING – BUT that is also their weakness! Attempting to test them scientifically is impossible and therefore pointless!

The Process of Science

Combining POPPER'S CRITERION with the generation of a Theory by INDUCTION – going from a specific instance to a general explanation – there is (arguably) a general process by which Science progresses.

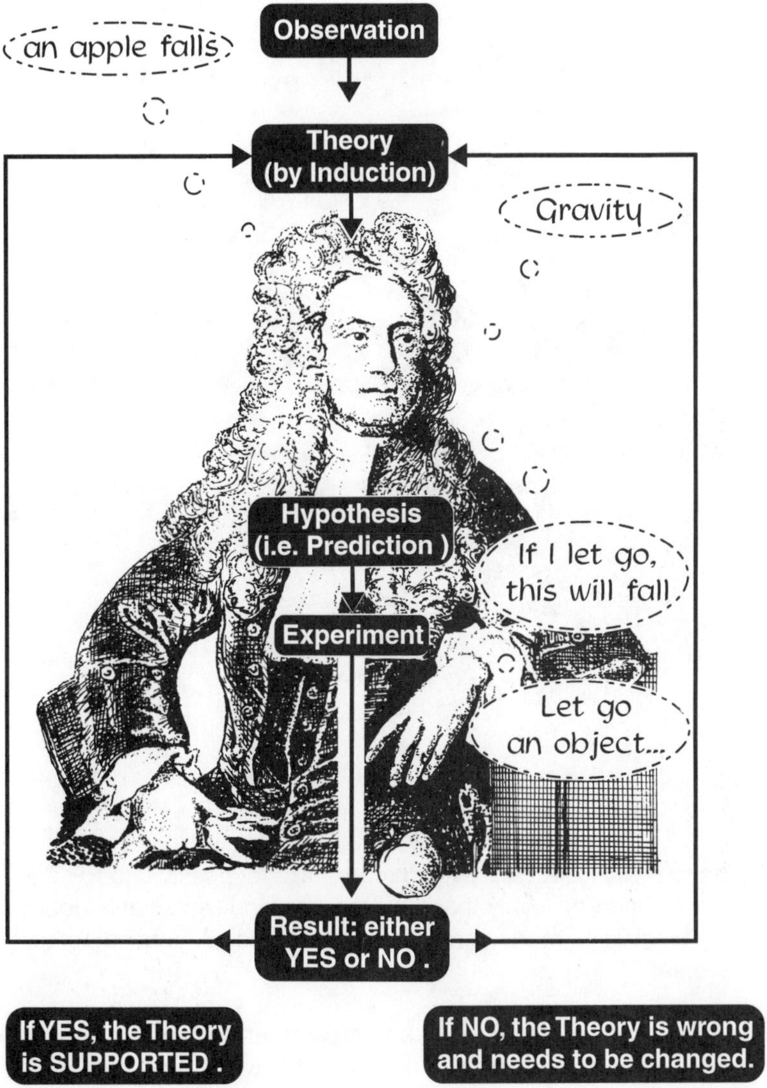

One very important aspect of this process is that a Theory can only be DISPROVED, it cannot be PROVED...

Why Can't Anything Be Proved?

Although we often use the word "prove" in everyday life, strictly speaking, NOTHING CAN BE PROVED. This is simply because NO amount of evidence is sufficient – there's always the possibility of new, conflicting, evidence.

So, just collecting lots of data to SUPPORT a Theory is of limited use: a good Scientist looks for evidence to DISPROVE a Theory.

Science is a bit like Law: even in court, it's not possible to PROVE someone is guilty – only that they are, "beyond reasonable doubt". There have been many convictions where later evidence has led to a reversal!

In Science, we can also never be certain that a Theory is "correct" or "true" – we therefore prefer to think of a Theory as being USEFUL, until a better one comes along. Newton's Theory of Gravity (attraction of objects) was replaced by Einstein's Theory of Gravity (distortions in space).

Nothing is Certain...

On an even deeper philosophical level, we can never be certain about the future anyway. Just because something's always happened in the past doesn't mean it will definitely happen in the future.

But it's relatively easy to predict the behaviour of chemicals – the probabilities involved are usually extremely high. People, on the other hand, tend to be much more unpredictable!

Probability in Psychology

As a "Rule of Thumb", Psychologists use 95% certainty as being acceptable. They allow a 5% chance of being wrong. If possible, they prefer 99% certainty, i.e. only 1% chance of being wrong. This is why Psychological research is usually expressed statistically....

In order to calculate such statistics, Psychologists use a variety of **statistical tests** – t-test, Wilcoxon, Mann-Whitney, Chi-squared, etc. – depending on the circumstances.

New students to the subject are often surprised, and sometimes initially put off, by these statistics – but they're essential to the scientific approach. Anyway, it's not necessary to know WHY these tests work, just that they do. Statistical tests are simply TOOLS to get the job done.

THE BIRTH OF PSYCHOLOGY

Psychology was officially born in 1879, when Wilhelm Wundt (1832-1920) opened the first recognized laboratory for the study of human behaviour in Leipzig, Germany. Wundt (pronounced "Voont", quickly) was the first to use the term "Experimental Psychology".

"My goal is to mark out a new domain of science!"
"The first step in the investigation of a fact must therefore be a description of the individual elements... of which it consists."
Principles of Physiological Psychology (1873-4)
Lectures on the Minds of Men and Animals (1863)

Wundt used INTROSPECTION – the examination of one's own mental state – training people to **introspect** using strict rules:

(1) observers must be able to determine when the process is to be introduced.
(2) they must be in a state of readiness or strained attention.
(3) it must be possible to repeat the observation several times.
(4) the experimental conditions must be capable of variation in terms of the controlled manipulation of the stimuli.

Critics were worried that intense self-observation would drive students insane!

Evaluation of Wundt

Wundt carefully organized the first experiments and also started Social ("Volk") Psychology, with inquiries into language, art, social customs, myths, laws and morals.

Wundt's fame spread quickly. His students set up their own labs on returning home – in the USA, Italy, Russia and Japan.

Wundt's topics are still studied today – the senses, estimation of time, reaction times, attention span, emotions, verbal associations.
However, Wundt's actual findings and theories are rarely used now, having been superseded by others. Introspection was abandoned for being too subjective.

Wundt's value is that he founded Psychology by rejecting the non-scientific thinking of the past.

BEFORE PSYCHOLOGY

The significance of Wundt was the new scientific approach. Previously, many of the same questions had been asked by philosophers, beginning with Socrates (470-399 BC) in ancient Greek times – on memory, learning, motivation, perception, dreaming, abnormal behaviour.

But the Greeks were often reluctant to MEASURE things. Plato and Aristotle both believed that the truth could be found through thinking rather than doing.

I believed that body and soul are separate.
I attacked your Dualism... created a whole system of knowledge... and described experiences, e.g. waking, sleeping, gender, memory, emotions, self-control, relationships...
Plato (c. 428-347 BC)
Aristotle (384-322 BC)

Aristotle's teachings dominated western philosophy in the medieval period of Christian theology. It could be said that Christianity's "psychology" was its preoccupation with sin, guilt, penance, and authority.

Descartes' Mind-Body Problem

The Philosopher who most directly contributed to Psychology was **René Descartes** (1596-1650). Descartes tackled the Mind-Body Problem in *Discourse on Method* (1637) and *The Meditations* (1641). Before Descartes it was mainly believed that the Mind and Body are distinct (Platonic Dualism), with the Mind influencing the Body BUT NOT the other way round.

According to Descartes, the Mind has a single function – **thought**. (Descartes' emphasis on reason is called "Rationalism".) Furthermore, the Mind produces 2 kinds of ideas.

"Derived Ideas arise from external stimuli on the senses – the sound of a bell, the sight of a tree."
"Innate Ideas come from the mind or consciousness – the self, perfection, infinity, God..."

This led to the **Nature-Nurture Debate** – whether certain behaviour is mainly inborn or learned. People believing more in "Nature" explanations became "Nativists" (although this term is not used much nowadays). On the other hand, some people emphasized Learning or "Nurture".

Associationism

John Locke (1632-1704), in *An Essay Concerning Human Understanding* (1690), rejected Descartes' innate ideas and agreed with Aristotle that the mind at birth is a *tabula rasa* ("clean slate").

"Let us then suppose the mind to be, as we say, white paper, void of all characters, without any ideas..."
"From where has it all the materials of reason and knowledge? To this I answer, in one word, from EXPERIENCE."

Locke formally began British Empiricism and produced a Theory of Association. Associationism was developed in the 18th century by Bishop Berkeley (1685-1753) and David Hume (1711-76).

According to Hume, we assume "cause and effect" associations through experiencing pairs of events, e.g. one billiard ball hitting another.

Transcendentalism

Immanuel Kant (1724-1804) turned Hume's Associationism on its head, saying already existing (i.e. "*a priori*") concepts of "cause" enable us to have objective experiences. Kant also argued that innate reason alone cannot explain what does or doesn't exist, which disagreed with Descartes' Rationalism. Consequently, Kant's *Critique of Pure Reason* (1781) presents the case for combining new experiences with existing ideas, i.e. "synthetic *a priori* propositions".

"David Hume... interrupted my dogmatic slumber"
"Pure intuition... of space and time... is *a priori*"
"The part is possible only through the whole, which is never the case with things in themselves."

Kant described three mental activities: Knowing, Feeling and Willing. Today, Psychologists often distinguish Knowledge ("Cognitive") from Emotional ("Affective") thoughts, for example when analyzing attitudes.

Kant's views were **transcendental** – that is, explanations outside particular experiences. Closely related were the "Idealism" (e.g. Hegel) and "Romanticism" (e.g. Schopenhauer, Kierkegaard) that developed in Germany – especially in the appreciative, mystical attitude towards nature. This contrasted with the mechanistic approach of others.

James Mill & J. S. Mill

The libertarian philosopher John Stuart Mill (1806-1873) was the son of James Mill (1773-1836), a **utilitarian** – one who believed in striving for "the greatest happiness of the greatest number".

James Mill (in *Analysis of the Phenomena of the Human Mind,* 1829) believed the mind to be passive, but J. S. Mill (in *Autobiography,* 1873 and *On Liberty,* 1859) disagreed...

J. S. Mill believed in "Mental Chemistry", especially "Creative Synthesis" – the fusion of sensory elements into new compounds which are more than the sum of the constituent parts. (This view, and the emphasis on the active mind, was later adopted by the Gestaltists.) J. S. Mill said Psychology could become a true science.

Comte's Positivism

Auguste Comte (1798-1857) was a friend and benefactor of J. S. Mill, but though he disagreed with Mill about the science of mind, he did believe in a science of society and is called "The Father of Sociology".

Comte's contribution to Psychology is through POSITIVISM.

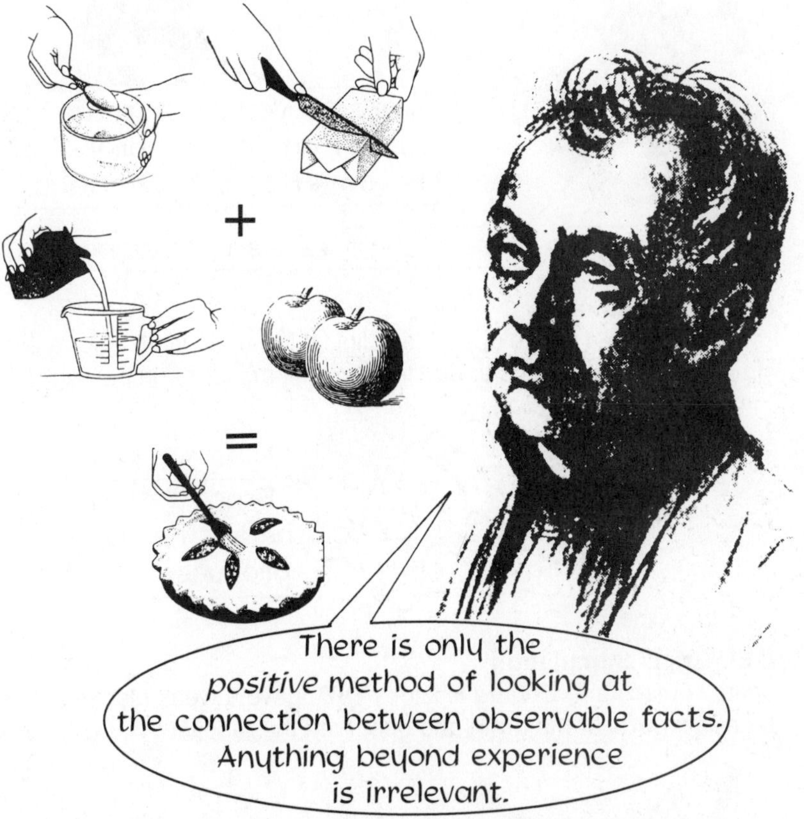

There is only the *positive* method of looking at the connection between observable facts. Anything beyond experience is irrelevant.

Positivism reduces propositions to simple facts – **Reductionism**. This later influenced Behaviourists and many Bio-Psychologists.

Comte's Positivism eventually led to the Logical Positivists of the 1920s (A. J. Ayer, etc.) who wanted to get rid of all statements that couldn't be publicly verified or empirically tested – a view many Psychologists strongly support today.

Early Brain Research Techniques

During the 1830s, **physiology** became an experimental discipline, especially through Johannes Müller (Berlin), Marshall Hall (London) and Pierre Flourens (Paris). They studied brain functions, trying to locate specialized areas and develop new techniques, still used today.

1. Extirpation
Hall and Flourens:

We removed or destroyed part of an animal's brain, to find the effects on behaviour.
Later, two more techniques were developed.

2. Clinical Method
Paul Broca (1861) developed the "Clinical Method", waiting for a patient with behaviour problems to die, then examining for brain damage.

Broca's Area in the left hemisphere produces speech.

3. Electrical Stimulation
Gustav Fritsch and Eduard Hitzig in 1870 gave a weak electrical current to certain parts of the brain and observed the reaction.

Notice the movement of legs...

These research techniques were very useful, but the important Big Theory was published by one man.

Darwin's Theory of Evolution

When **Charles Darwin** (1809-82) published *On The Origin Of Species By Natural Selection* (1859), it caused a storm – publicly and intellectually. Much of the immediate reaction was simply due to misunderstandings and ignorance about what he really said. (Which still continues!) There isn't so much *one* theory of evolution but a set of 4 sub-theories.

The first is **Species Change.** Over time and generations, physical (and behavioural) characteristics alter. See the fossil evidence...
The second is **Gradual Change.** Alterations occur in small steps, over many generations. Although many "steps" in the fossil records are missing.
The third is **Common Descent.** Organisms can be traced back to their ancestors – like a giant family tree.

Now let's look at the fourth and most important sub-theory, **Natural Selection**...

Natural Selection

Natural Selection comes in two parts. First, changes can occur from one generation to the next. This is now known to be **random** "mutations" in the genes – for example, those caused by natural radiation. (Darwin didn't know *why* changes occurred, just that they did.)

Second, there is the **meaning** of "Selection":

> Changes that are beneficial give the new individual a better chance to survive. Conversely, adverse genetic changes give less chance of survival.

I used evolution to explain why there are so *many* variations in the same species...

Take the case of finches from the Pacific. Neighbouring islands had different food: some had plenty of nuts but few insects, whereas others had more insects but few nuts. When mutation created birds with *large* bills the "nut" islands enabled them to survive, while the thin-billed birds there died out. BUT birds mutating with *thin* bills were able to survive on the "insect" islands, where the larger-billed died out. Where animals fit into the environment in this way is called **Survival of the fittest**.

The Importance of Evolution

The concept of "Survival of the fittest" helps explain the variety and distribution of living organisms, both alive and dead. (Important: it does *not* mean "fit" as in "strong and healthy"! Many small, weak creatures survive while the large, strong dinosaurs have all died out!)

Since Darwin, evolution has been witnessed many times in action, e.g. the Peppered Moth, which has mutated into two versions – with "Light" or "Dark" wing patterns.

Tree with lichen, before pollution.

Originally, the "Dark" version didn't survive as well, due to the lack of camouflage against trees with light-coloured lichen. "Light" versions were consequently more common.

Tree without lichen, after pollution.

However, where pollution destroyed lichen (revealing dark plain bark beneath), the "Light" variations became much more vulnerable while the "Dark" became camouflaged.

Evolution Today

In recent years, we've witnessed bacteria and viruses mutating and becoming resistant to such drugs as antibiotics. And some viruses having no known cure, for instance, HIV causing AIDS.

Thus, evolution can be observed in action today!

Evolution isn't just the backbone of biology, explaining the structure and function of living creatures, it's also very useful to Psychologists explaining such behaviour as courtship rituals and territory defence. Richard Dawkins has used it (with important modifications) to explain **altruism** – helping others without apparent personal benefit – so the genes survive (*The Selfish Gene*, Dawkins, 1976). Dawkins is also often misunderstood!

Galton's Contributions

Francis Galton (1822-1911), Darwin's cousin, was keen on evolution and heredity. He founded "Individual Differences" and discovered the uniqueness of finger-prints (1892). Galton was also an obsessive counter and measurer. He even counted yawns and coughs at lectures and theatres – trying to produce a "boredom measure"!

Galton set up a laboratory in 1884, at the International Health Exhibition, that continued for 6 years in the South Kensington Museum.

I collected data from over 9,000 people who paid to be measured on height, weight strength, hearing, vision, etc.

Galton used and developed 3 particular statistical measurements: **Probability**, **Normal Distribution** and **Correlation**. Galton's *Hereditary Genius* (1869) and *English Men of Science* (1874) contained many case studies of famous judges, doctors and scientists who were born into families with corresponding talents. From this research, Galton calculated the high PROBABILITY that eminent men will father eminent sons.

The Normal Distribution

Galton used the NORMAL DISTRIBUTION CURVE developed by **Adolphe Quetelet** (Belgium, 1796-1874) – for example, the distribution of people's height.

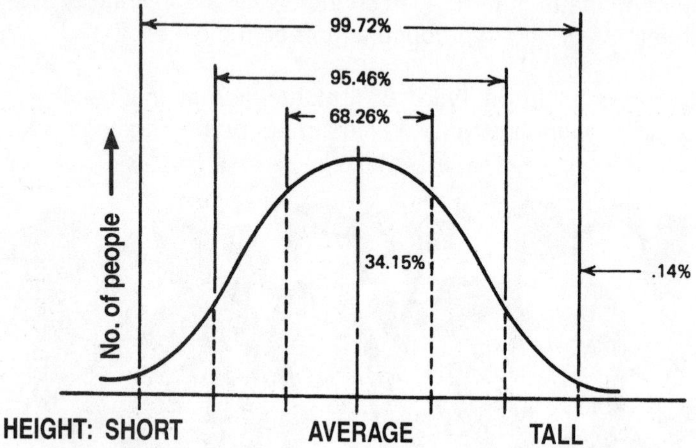

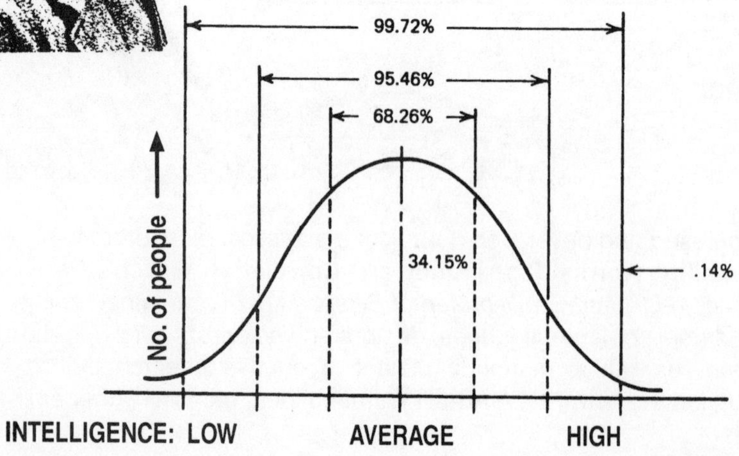

Correlations

Galton published *Correlations* (1888) which illustrated relationships graphically – for instance, that tall men are not as tall as their fathers and short men are taller than their fathers.

This also demonstrated the principle of "regression to the mean".
average man

Galton's student, Karl Pearson, developed his tutor's formula for calculating correlation (on a scale of - 1.0 to + 1.0): "The Pearson Correlation Coefficient", used extensively today.

Using **statistics**, Galton came down firmly on the Nature side of the Nature-Nurture debate. In many ways, Galton had a greater influence than even Wundt did.

Structuralism and Functionalism

Germany (even though not unified until 1870) was the Mother of Psychology. It provided the right empirical and positivistic *Zeitgeist* – the intellectual and economic environment, with many Universities in contrast to England's TWO! Leading up to 1879, three other physiologists assisted Wundt: Helmholtz, Weber, and Fechner. Afterwards, although Wundt dominated, other researchers produced parallel contributions – especially **Ebbinghaus**, Muller, Brentano, Stumpf, and Kulpe. But it was Wundt's most famous student who took Psychology to the USA.

Edward Titchener (1867-1927), an English student and translator of Wundt, went to the United States (1893) to set up his own laboratory at Cornell. (Oxford refused: no Psychology until 1936!) He claimed to be an ardent follower of Wundt, but soon developed his own approach.

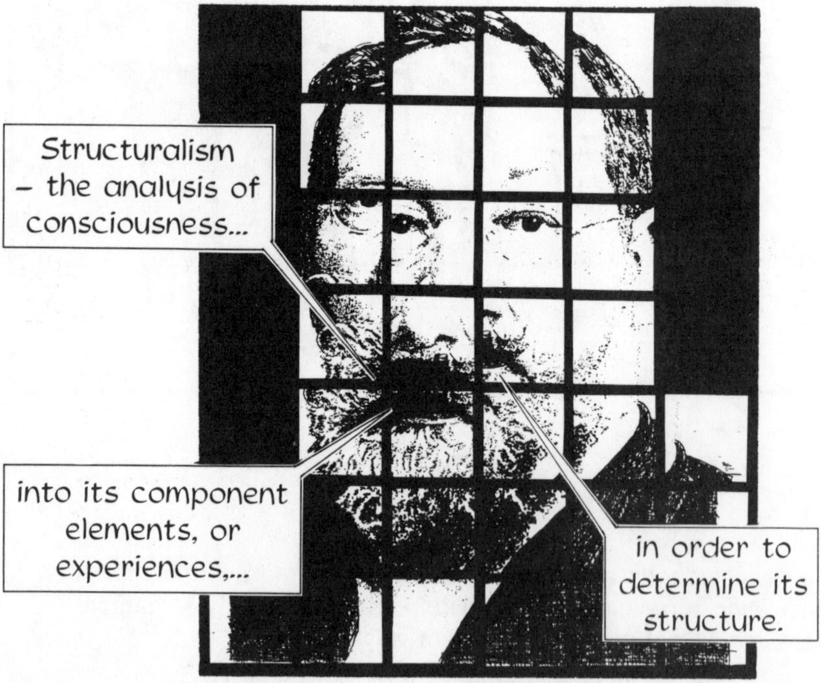

This was still too introspective, and mechanistic - dividing into elements experiences that only make sense as wholes (as the Gestaltists later argued). Structuralism lasted about 25 years, then ended when Titchener died, but it was on its way out anyway.

The immediate opposition came from **Functionalism.** As it suggests, this concerned the way the mind FUNCTIONS. The immediate background was Darwin and Galton's consciousness, and Herbert Spencer (1820-1903, another Englishman) who invented Social Darwinism. (Spencer wore earmuffs to stop his thoughts from being disrupted!)

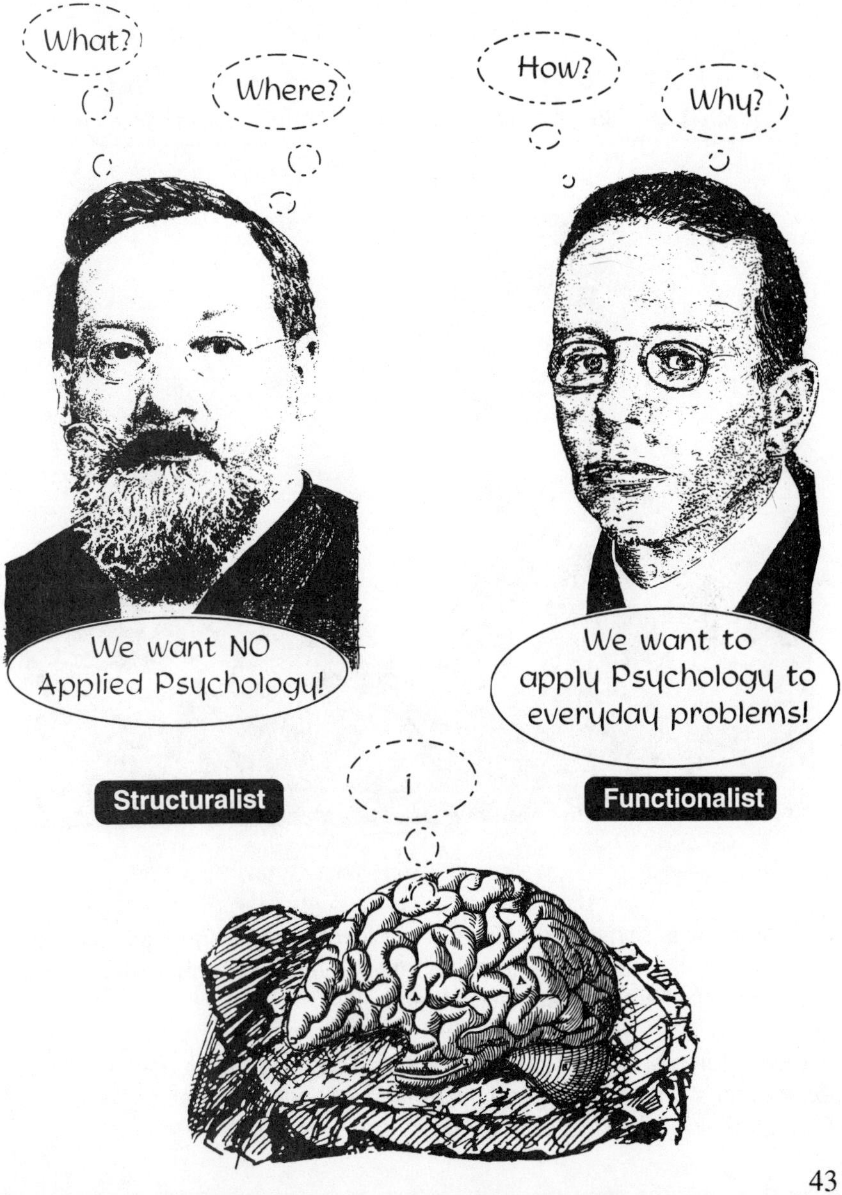

What?
Where?
How?
Why?
We want NO Applied Psychology!
We want to apply Psychology to everyday problems!
Structuralist
Functionalist
!

The First Functionalists

William James (1842-1910) taught America's first Psychology course in 1875. However, he wasn't keen on experiments! He was interested in consciousness as a product of the brain's activities, coining the phrase "Stream of Consciousness" to describe the continuous, flowing *process* (not elements).

But James was considered non-scientific and unconventional: studying telepathy, clairvoyance, spiritualism, etc. – the very things from which most scientists were dissociating themselves!

James' interests, though, were appealing (such as "religious experiences"), and he began important applications, notably Educational Psychology with *Talks to Teachers* (1899).

Education was also a major interest of **John Dewey** (1859-1952)* who published America's first textbook, *Psychology* in 1886, soon eclipsed by James'. He disliked "dichotomies" – he wouldn't separate mind-body, means-ends, fact-value, thought-action, individual-society. Instead, he was **pragmatic** (like James), that is, he favoured whatever works effectively in practice.

Dewey was keen on Evolution: people struggle to survive. He concentrated on education (1904).

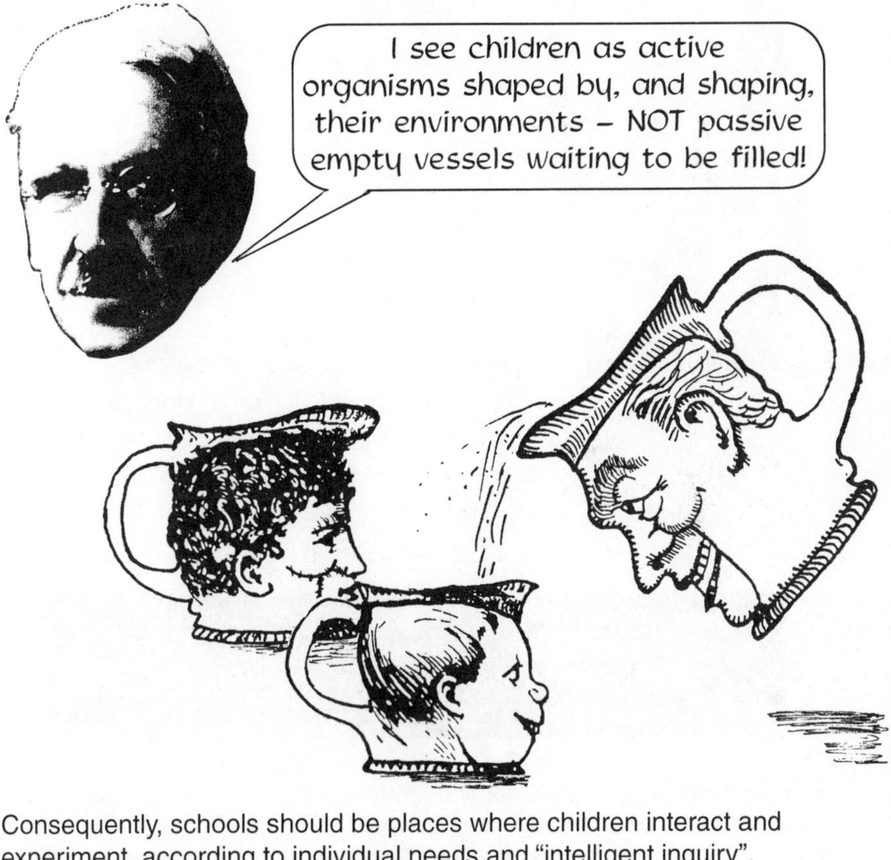

I see children as active organisms shaped by, and shaping, their environments – NOT passive empty vessels waiting to be filled!

Consequently, schools should be places where children interact and experiment, according to individual needs and "intelligent inquiry". Thus, Dewey founded "progressive education" .

* Not Melville Dewey, the librarian (1851-1931) who invented the *Dewey Decimal System* of library classification. (Psychology is "150".)

James Angell (1869-1949), a student of John Dewey and colleague of William James, formally turned Functionalism into a school of thought – "The Chicago School". Angell's book *Psychology* (1904) was extremely successful.

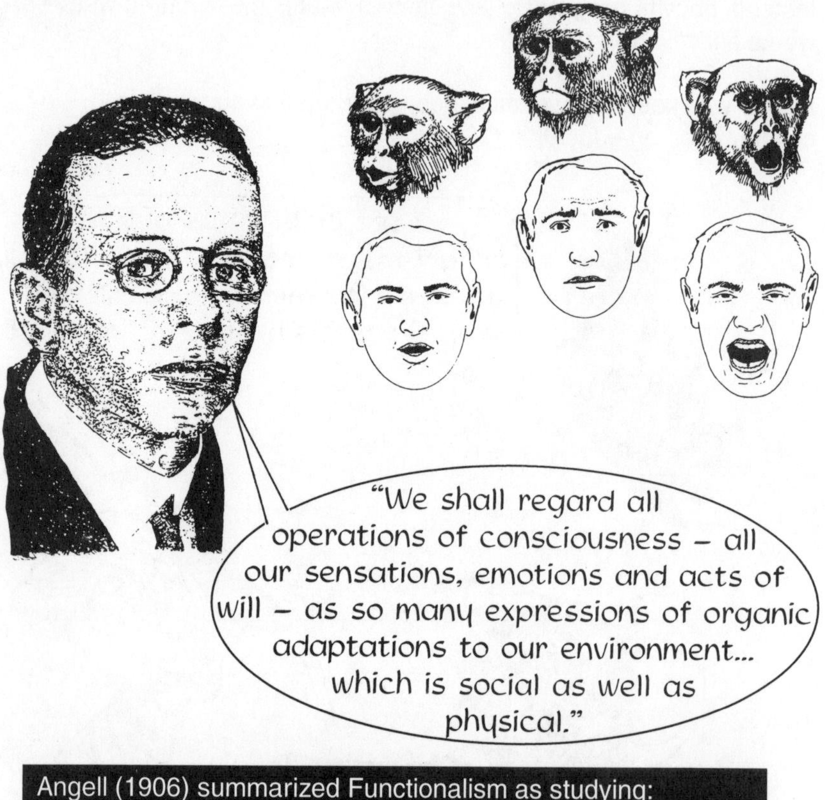

"We shall regard all operations of consciousness – all our sensations, emotions and acts of will – as so many expressions of organic adaptations to our environment... which is social as well as physical."

Angell (1906) summarized Functionalism as studying:
(1) mental operations, not elements
(2) consciousness, including processes like willing and judging
(3) no mind-body distinction

Harvey Carr (1873-1954) succeeded from about 1919, i.e. when Functionalism was already moving away from the (subjective) mind and consciousness, towards studying (objective) behaviour. Functionalism finally ended when it lost the need to fight: in a sense, everyone became a "Functionalist". (Although few call themselves that today.)

Historically, Functionalism was an important bridge between Structuralism and Behaviourism – and the other current Perspectives.

THE PERSPECTIVES

The first two perspectives gave way to the six we have today (although the true Cognitive and Humanistic “Schools” didn’t arrive until the 1950s and ’60s).

The historical development can be seen as follows.

TIME CHART

Structuralism	1890s	('20s)
Functionalism	1906	
Perspectives: (“Schools”)		
Psychodynamic	1896	
Behaviourism	1913	
Gestalt/Cognitive	1912	1960
(“Non-schools”)		
Humanistic	1950s	
Bio-Psychology	1880s	
Social-Cultural	1880s	

The first three Perspectives are often also called “Schools” because they each consisted of a group of people with reasonably uniform ideas.

The last three can’t meaningfully be called “Schools”, since they don’t have such groups of people in agreement. However, they broadly represent important ways of thinking.

1. THE PSYCHODYNAMIC PERSPECTIVE

"Psychodynamic" means "active mind". There is mental struggle – especially in the hidden **unconscious** mind. In practice, this often simply means applying the **Psychoanalytic theories** of Freud and, to a greater or lesser extent, followers and dissenters such as Jung, Adler, Erikson, Klein, Lacan... depending on your personal favourites!

But **Sigmund Freud** (1856-1939) started it all by coining the term **Psychoanalysis** (1896) to describe his theories and techniques for finding and curing the mental problems of his patients.

Lie down and relax...
Just say whatever comes into your mind...

But Freud wasn't only interested in mental disorders: he spent his life trying to produce a coherent set of theories to explain ALL human behaviour. He never achieved his goal of One Grand Theory, so it's easiest to think of separate but inter-related theories. There are five particularly important ones.

1. Conscious / Pre-Conscious / Unconscious Mind

Freud described this using the analogy of an iceberg, which isn't really adequate (since it implies something rigid rather than fluid) but it's a start...

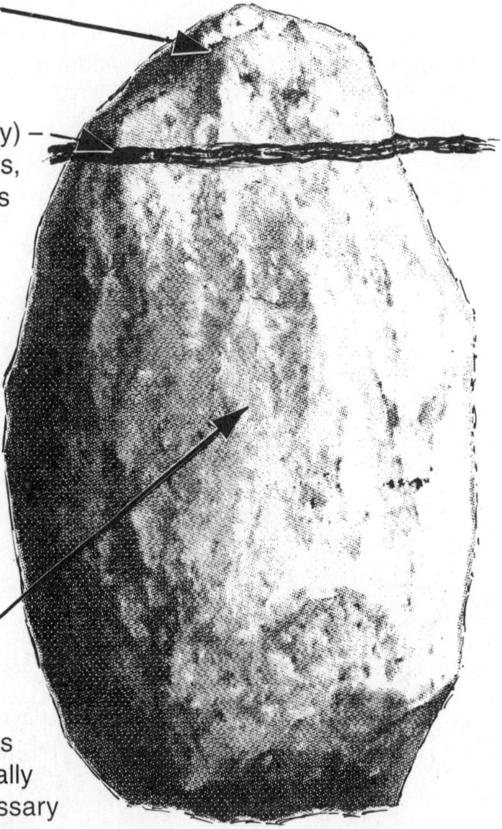

The Conscious (top 1/7th) – the awareness we have when we are awake.

The Pre-Conscious (boundary) – containing memories of dreams, "Slips of the tongue", etc. Gives clues about the Unconscious from thoughts and actions that appear there. If you remember a dream, you are not directly revealing unconscious thoughts but recalling highly coded ideas. This symbolism protects us, so we are not upset or disturbed by what our Unconscious is REALLY thinking!

The Unconscious (6/7th) – containing secret wishes and fears; traumatic memories of the past, etc. All these thoughts are completely hidden and totally unavailable to us. This is necessary for survival – forgetting past traumas in order to get on with our lives. We can NEVER directly see into the Unconscious.

In strict Freudian terms, it's wrong to say "Subconscious" when referring to the Unconscious. He was adamant that it's totally unseen and unknown.

2. The Libido

"Libido" is often used today to mean "sex drive", but this is a corruption or, at least, over-simplification of Freud's meaning. It is the INBORN ENERGY we have that motivates and enables us to survive – sexual activity is one manifestation.

Freud used the Steam Engine Model to describe this.

The level of Libido ("steam") we are born with is a central aspect of our personalities. Some people are born with more than others. How we use that energy also depends on our personalities (needs and desires) and our activities (work, hobbies, interests).

3. The Id, Ego and Superego

The mind has three parts, each with its own motives and developmental progress but, usually, they combine to help us survive.

The Id develops first. It is inborn and alone for a couple of years. It operates by **The Pleasure Principle** – the baby seeks pleasure (e.g. drink, food, warmth, comfort) and avoids the unpleasurable (e.g. hunger, being wet and cold). The Id is selfish and typically wants *immediate gratification*.

The Ego develops from about 2 years and operates by **The Reality Principle**. To survive, we must sometimes be realistic and plan for the future. Thus, the Id can't always be allowed its own way, so the Ego often has to battle with *it*. (Id is Latin for *it* – Freud used the German "*das es*", translated as Id.)

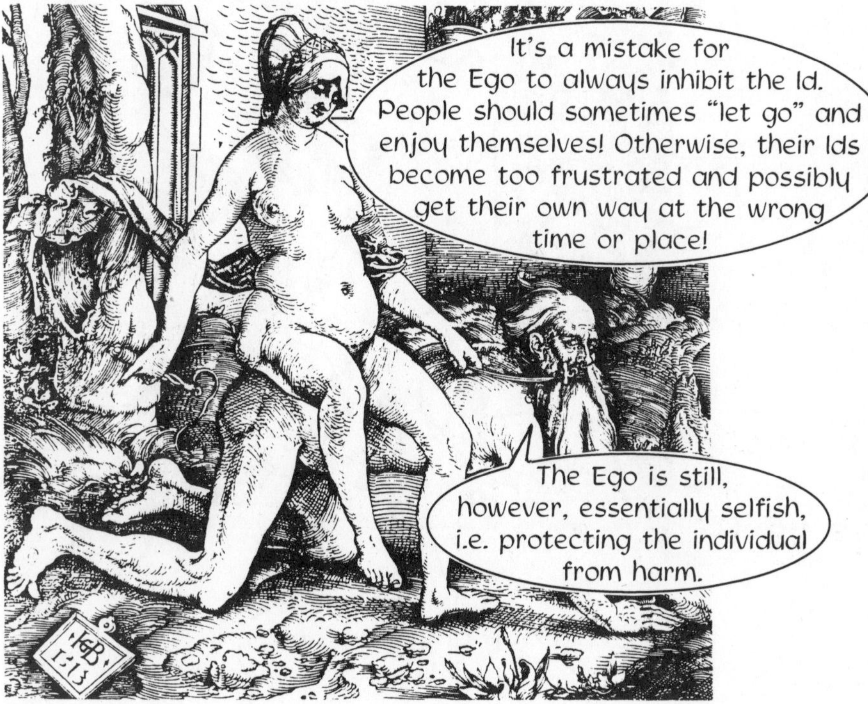

It's a mistake for the Ego to always inhibit the Id. People should sometimes "let go" and enjoy themselves! Otherwise, their Ids become too frustrated and possibly get their own way at the wrong time or place!
The Ego is still, however, essentially selfish, i.e. protecting the individual from harm.

Freud thought this was particularly a problem for people brought up in restrictive Europe, where enjoyment – especially sexual – was often inhibited.

The Superego starts to develop about age three (influenced by parents), then gradually develops throughout childhood, becoming fully mature after puberty.

"Super" means "above" – looking down and monitoring the "Id-Ego" battle.

The Superego is the "conscience" or "moral watchdog" that stops us from doing wrong, especially in the sense of being anti-social. Whereas the Id and Ego are selfish, the Superego considers others too.

Applied to criminal behaviour, it may well be that some individuals never fully develop a Superego. This could account for those who show no guilt or remorse for their crimes.

4. The Stages of Psychosexual Development

Freud described 5 stages we all pass through:

Oral (0-2 yrs)
Anal (2-3 yrs)
Phallic (3-6 yrs)
Latent (6-11 yrs)
Genital (11 + yrs)

The first three stages are particularly important for personality development.

The Oral Stage (0-2 yrs)

The mouth is the prime source of pleasure, for survival: the baby instinctively sucks. Through oral satisfaction, the baby develops trust and an optimistic personality.

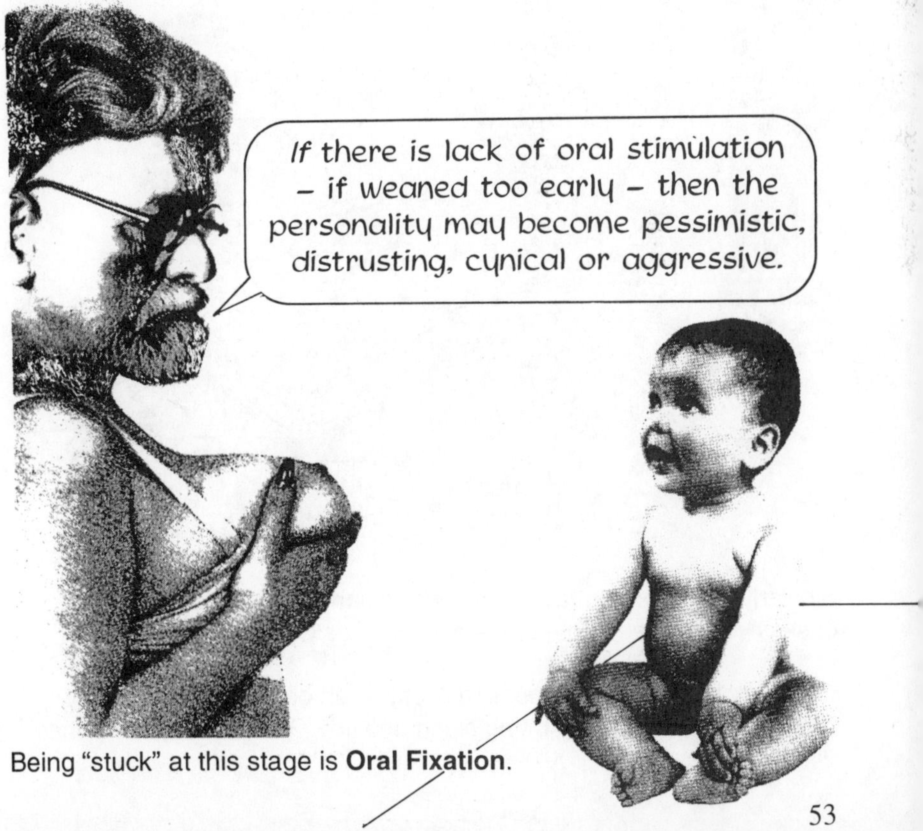

If there is lack of oral stimulation – if weaned too early – then the personality may become pessimistic, distrusting, cynical or aggressive.

Being "stuck" at this stage is **Oral Fixation**.

The Anal Stage (2-3 yrs)

The focus of pleasure shifts to the anus, helping the child become aware of its bowels and how to control them, aiding "potty training" – going to the toilet in the right place and time. Parents should encourage regularity and hygiene. By deciding itself, the child takes an important step of independence, developing confidence and a sense of when to "give things up". However, over-strictness about forcing the child to "go", or about timing or cleanliness, can cause personality problems – depending on how it reacts...

Examples of Anal Fixation

Forcing the child to "go" may cause reluctance about giving away ANYTHING. The person may become a hoarder or a miser – classic **Anal Retention**!

Similarly, over-concern about "going regularly" may cause either obsessive time-keeping – or the type who's always late.

Over-emphasis on cleanliness may cause an obsessive personality, always concerned about being clean and tidy. Or, rebelling, someone who's always untidy.

The Phallic Stage (3-6 yrs)

Children become aware of their genitals ("playing with themselves") and sexual differences. Consequently, development is different for boys and girls.

The Oedipus Complex

Each boy, unconsciously, goes through a sequence of sub-stages:
(a) Developing a strong desire for his mother.
(b) Noticing the close bond between his parents (sleeping together).
(c) Becoming jealous of his father and hating him.
(d) Being afraid of his father, who might discover his true feelings (i.e. the boy's desire, jealousy and hatred)
(e) Fearing the ultimate punishment for a boy – CASTRATION!

At this point, the poor boy is in despair and desperate to resolve it.

Resolution of the Oedipus Complex occurs on route to "normality". The boy has to **identify** with, that is become like, his father. This solves the problem because being like the father means (a) the father will like him, and therefore won't punish him; (b) the mother will also like him!

Identification causes the boy to take on his father's attitudes, moral beliefs (Superego development) and gender roles.

Since her mother is the same, the girl also ends up "identifying", i.e. adopting her morality and gender roles. (This was always rather vague!).

*After working closely with Freud, 1906-13, Jung decided there was too much emphasis on sex. So he split from Freud and produced his own "Jungian" concepts: **introversion** and **extraversion**, **complexes**, **archetypes** and the **collective unconscious**.

5. The Defence Mechanisms

These are ways to unconsciously protect ourselves from unpleasant ideas. In small doses, they help everyday survival. However, over-use causes problems.
Two have been mentioned – **Fixation** and **Identification**.

Here are some more on this page and the next.

Repression: pushing down unwanted ideas into the Unconscious and keeping them there. This avoids being reminded of horrible memories, or things we fear, or wishes we feel guilty about. Too much Repression can be exhausting. It takes energy (Libido) to keep Unconscious thoughts hidden.

Sometimes, therefore, it's better for the unpleasant ideas to rise into the Conscious mind to be confronted and dealt with.
The psychoanalyst's job is to trace these troublesome traumas, help make them conscious, and assist the patient in facing them.

Regression means going back to an earlier stage. It's natural to seek situations that give comfort, especially when under stress. Sucking a finger, thumb, pencil, sweet, cigarette, drink etc, is **Oral Regression.**

The need to stimulate the mouth.

If something frustrates, for example, or someone annoys, then we may "take it out" on someone else.

Displacement means diverting your energy (Libido) into another activity. This is often because we can't, or don't want to, do something.

Sublimation is the name given to Displacement that's "healthy" – getting rid of stress or anger by doing sport, digging the garden, etc.

Other Defence Mechanisms include: **Denial**, **Projection**, and so on.

Freud's Evidence

Where did Freud get his evidence? Mostly from "talking sessions" with his patients (like Anna O, Little Hans, The Rat Man) which he then wrote up as "case studies". These read more like stories than empirical findings.

Freud's methods have been adapted by subsequent analysts, therapists and Psychiatrists.

Post-Freudians include: Alfred Adler (1870-1937), Carl Jung (1875-1961), Karen Horney (1885-1952), Erich Fromm (1900-1980), Erik Erikson (1902-94).

Evaluation of Freud

Freud cured many patients, or at least helped them understand and cope with their problems, and his methods are still used in Psychiatry today.

Freud had an enormous effect on modern societies, fundamentally changing the ways people think about themselves and others.

In Psychology, however, Freud is still highly controversial. Many Psychologists dismiss him for being "unscientific" or "untestable" as Popper would say. Consequently, a lot of Degree courses contain little Freudian theory, or miss it out entirely! Many Psychologists prefer to stick with what is easily observable and measurable – **behaviour**.

2. THE PERSPECTIVE OF BEHAVIOURISM

The roots of Behaviourism can be found in the philosophical idea of **Associationism.** Associationism, in its simplest form, is the study of how ideas get linked together, and trying to find "laws" that describe and explain behaviour. (However, it was never a "School" – just a principle.) Associationism developed out of the British Empiricist movement (as we've seen, Locke, Berkeley, and Hume), although its roots go back to Aristotle.

Certain key Psychologists used Associationism to explain **learning**, a topic central to Psychology.

What is "learning"?

Learning is a relatively permanent **change in behaviour** due to experience.

("Relatively permanent change" excludes temporary changes, such as illness, tiredness, getting drunk, etc. "Experience" excludes changes due to genetic inheritance, maturation, permanent injury, etc.)

Learning Theory - Classical Conditioning

Ivan Pavlov (1849-1936), a Russian physiologist who founded the Institute of Experimental Medicine in 1890, studied digestion. He published *Lectures on the Work of the Digestive Glands* in 1897.

From 1901, I studied the way laboratory dogs would learn (be "conditioned") to salivate without food...
When I heard dishes rattled or saw an assistant.

Let's see what his famous experiment was about...

Pavlov's Famous Experiment

The dog was harnessed in a sound-proof, smell-proof cubicle, so it could not see, hear or smell the assistants(!). A sound was made when food was given, and the amount of salivation was measured. After several such pairings (**trials**), the sound was made WITHOUT food – but the dog STILL salivated!

SOUND – a Neutral Stimulus that becomes a Conditioned Stimulus

CONTROLLED ENVIRONMENT

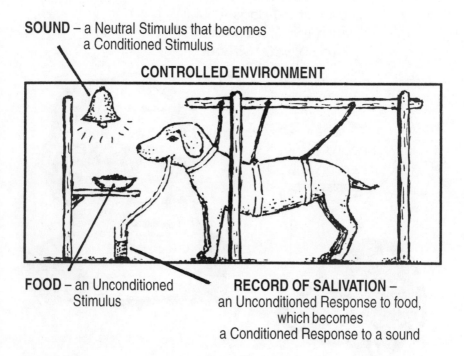

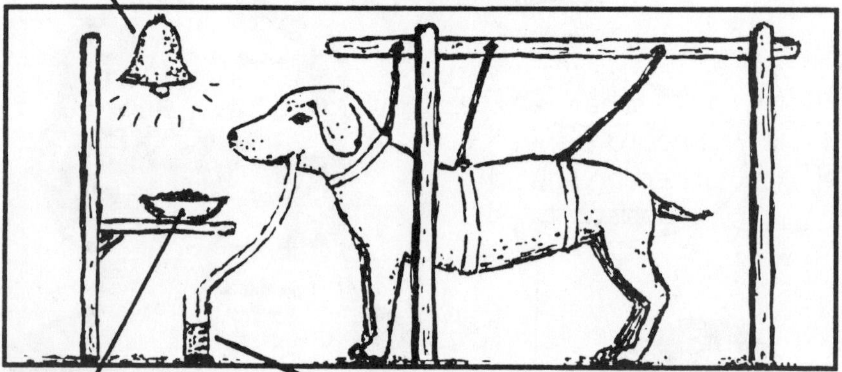

FOOD – an Unconditioned Stimulus

RECORD OF SALIVATION – an Unconditioned Response to food, which becomes a Conditioned Response to a sound

The whole process can be shown as follows:

BEFORE	DURING	AFTER
🔔 → no response	🔔 ⋱	🔔 ↘
(NS)	(NS)	(CS)
food → salivation	food → salivation	salivation
(US) (UR)	(US) (UR)	(CR)

In this way, Pavlov conditioned the dog to salivate whenever the sound was made.

Further Experiments

Pavlov found that when the CS (sound) was presented repeatedly without the US (food), the CR (salivation) gradually ceased – it became EXTINCT. (The response, not the dog!) During EXTINCTION, the dog often became drowsy or even fell asleep.

After some time (a day or two), when the CS (sound) was presented again, the CR (salivation) would start again, even though no US (food) was present. This was SPONTANEOUS RECOVERY.

Pavlov also found that the dog would respond to similar sounds...

"When conditioned to one definite tone... many of the other sounds produce the same conditioned reaction... this is known as GENERALIZATION."
NOBEL PRIZE 1904
"We then began a differentiation of a circle from an ellipse... i.e. the appearance of the circle was accompanied each time by feeding..."
"...whereas that of the ellipse was not. In this way DISCRIMINATION was obtained."
CIRCLE
ELLIPSE

Behaviour Therapy

What's the use of getting a dog to dribble? Although Pavlov's early experiments may seem unglamorous and even trivial, they are extremely important for two main reasons.

(1) Classical Conditioning explains virtually all learning that involves REFLEXES – heart-rate, perspiration, muscle-tension, etc.

(2) Since the above group of reflexes are signs of excitement – including FEAR and SEX – they may explain unusual and undesirable behaviour, e.g. PHOBIAS and SEXUAL DEVIATION. Consequently, Classical Conditioning is the basis of BEHAVIOUR THERAPY.

For example, using the "Before – During – After" diagram, it's possible to explain how phobias like arachnaphobia may have started.

BEFORE	DURING	AFTER
spider → no response (NS) story → fear (US) (UR)	(NS) ⇢ fear story → fear (US) (UR)	(CS) → fear (CR)

Little Miss Muffet
Sat on her tuffet
Eating her curds and whey
Down came a SPIDER
Who sat down beside her
And FRIGHTENED
Miss Muffet away!

(Note: If the response is strong, animals and humans can even be conditioned by ONE TRIAL LEARNING!)

Using this theoretical approach, several therapies have been developed.

(1) Desensitization Therapy

(Developed by J. Wolpe, 1958.)

This is based on gradually reducing the bond between the STIMULUS (e.g. spider) and RESPONSE (e.g. fear) by slowly introducing the STIMULUS and getting the phobic to relax.

(2) Counter Conditioning Therapy

Therapy can alternatively be based on replacing the S-R bond with a new bond, e.g. replacing "Spider – Fear" with "Spider – Happy", by introducing something pleasant (such as food) along with the spider.

Therapies can be combined – the **eclectic** approach.

(3) Aversion Therapy

This is also replacing one bond with another, but here replacing "nice" with "nasty", e.g. an emetic to cause vomiting.

For example, to stop habits such as smoking or alcoholism...

BEFORE	DURING	AFTER
smoking → pleasant emetic → vomitting	smoking ⋱ emetic → vomitting	smoking ↘ feeling sick

This technique can be used for any undesirable behaviour involving reflexes – from eating junk food to sexual deviancy (e.g. paedophilia).

Sexual Deviancy

Classical Conditioning can explain unusual sexual behaviour. Let's take the example of someone wearing rubber boots. How can this become **fetishism**?

BEFORE	DURING	AFTER
boots → no response	boots ↘	boots ↘
sexual stimulation → sexual response	sexual stimulation → sexual response	sexual response

Such conditioning could also include other details. If the boots are muddy, then mud may also later cause sexual excitement! This OBJECT has become sexually conditioned, a **fetish**. Literally ANY object can be conditioned in this way. Clothing is a common fetish, or materials (lace, silk, rubber, leather, etc). As with all conditioning, the more sexual experiences that are paired with the object(s), the more the Fetish will be reinforced and get stronger.

Voyeurism

Thus, Classical Conditioning can explain **all** forms of sexual deviation, both how it starts and why it continues. For instance, **voyeurism**: a person sexually aroused when watching other people.

Looking at pornography, in magazines or videos, is a form of voyeurism.

Mental Health Warning:
ALL sexual activities can be highly addictive. (Men are more prone due to the relative speed of arousal and satisfaction.)

Sadism and Masochism

Sadism is sexual pleasure from inflicting physical or mental suffering, named after the Marquis De Sade (1740-1814) – who, eventually, could only get satisfaction by causing pain.

It's possible, of course, for different deviations to be combined. Bondage (being tied up) and fetishism often accompany sadism and masochism.

Paedophilia

This is sexual excitement in the presence of children and is generally illegal. (Definitions vary: the age of consent in Spain and Holland is only 12 years.)

Paedophiles can be treated using a combination of therapies, including Aversion and Counter-Conditioning.

Homosexuality

This was once (e.g. in 1950s' America) seen as a "deviation" that could be "cured" in the same way as, for example, paedophilia. Such "therapies" were abandoned.

Thorndike and Connectionism

Just before the time that Pavlov was working in the USSR, **Edward Thorndike** in the USA (1874-1949) was independently working on "connectionism", another form of **associationism**.

I tested cats, timing how long it took each one to escape from a "Puzzle Box".
A cage with a pull-cord inside that unlocks the door.

Animal Intelligence: An experimental study of the associative processes in animals (1898)

The first time the cat escaped by **Trial and Error**, trying various actions, until it accidentally pressed the lever. After several trials, it would soon ASSOCIATE pressing the lever with escaping. Thorndike found that, on average, cats would initially take some time to escape, but with practice they soon learned to get out quickly.

Learning Curves and Laws

Thorndike plotted the time for the cats to escape on a graph, producing a "learning curve".

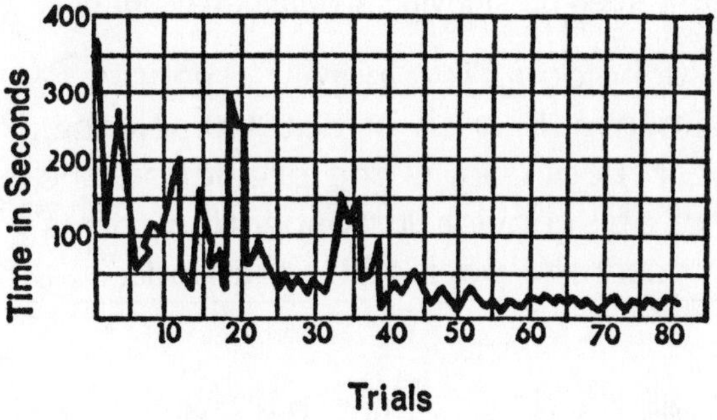

Similar curves can be drawn for humans learning anything...

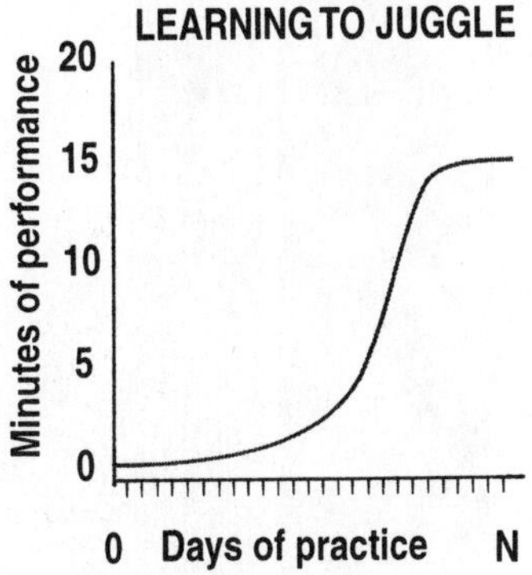

(A "steep learning curve" actually means that the individual has learned quickly!)

Thorndike produced two "laws" of learning:

(1) The Law of Exercise – repetition strengthens learning. (Or, "Practice makes perfect".) Learning poetry, lines of a play, math's tables by repetition is called **Rote Learning** or "Parrot Fashion".

(2) The Law of Effect – the effect of reward is to strengthen learning. (Or, "If it's pleasurable, it will be repeated".) Thorndike found reward (law 2) to be more effective than mere repetition (law 1).

Out of Associationism grew a whole new School.

Watson's Behaviourism

John B. Watson (1878-1958) crystallized contemporary trends and founded Behaviourism in *Psychology as the Behavorist views it* (1913). He was particularly keen on studying animal behaviour.

"Psychology... is a purely objective experimental branch of natural science. Its theoretical goal is the prediction and control of behavior. Introspection forms no essential part of its methods."

Not everyone liked this new approach: opponents included Titchener and McDougall. However, generally, Watson was very popular. His extreme "nurture" approach – denying the existence of ANY inherited characteristics – fitted the American *Zeitgeist*. People can be trained to be whatever they want.

Watson's Experiment

Watson's new approach rejected consciousness. He said emotions are simply environmental STIMULI and internal measurable RESPONSES, e.g. pulse rate, perspiration, blushing.

> Watson believed infants show 3 basic emotions:
> **fear** - caused by loud noise, sudden loss of support
> **rage** - caused by restriction of body movement
> **love** - caused by caressing and rocking
> Other emotions are compounds of these.

Watson's famous emotional study (1920) was of 11 month-old Albert who was shown a white rat, which he wasn't afraid of, and given a loud noise from behind – by hitting a steel bar with a hammer.

Watson argued that many adult fears and anxieties stem from similar childhood experiences.

So did Watson then cure Albert?

No. According to Watson, Albert was no longer available. Also, shortly after this, Watson was forced to permanently resign from academic life, because of the scandalous adultery with his assistant. From 1921, Watson was employed in advertising.

I spent the rest of my life applying Behaviourism to the prediction and control of consumer behaviour.
Psychologists have been involved in advertising ever since...
Make them dissatisfied with what they've got... make them desire the new product!
Dependable as the doctor himself
THE dependability of the Ford car—like that of the family physician who uses it so extensively—has become almost traditional.
Instinctively you place a trust in this car rarely, if ever, felt even for a larger, higher-powered automobile. And it is not uncommon to expect from it a far more difficult service.
Such universal faith is the result of Ford reliability proved over a long period of years—years in which quality has grown consistently better, while price has been steadily reduced.
RUNABOUT, $260; TOURING, $290; COUPE, $520; TUDOR SEDAN, $580; FORDOR SEDAN $660
All prices F. O. B. Detroit
On Open Cars Starter and Demountable Rims $85 Extra
Full-Size Balloon Tires Optional—Closed Cars $25; Open Cars $45
FORD MOTOR COMPANY, DETROIT, MICHIGAN
Ford
THE UNIVERSAL CAR

Ethics

We don't know what happened to Albert – but his case is one reason, of many, why there are now strict ethical guidelines that don't allow such research any more! Interestingly, even before the Ethics Codes came in during the 1950s, there were apparently no successful attempts at replicating Watson's study anyway!

Peter and the rabbit

However, some good things did come out of this. **Mary Cover Jones** (1896-1987), hearing about the Albert case, managed to "uncondition" an existing fear of rabbits in a boy named Peter. (Jones, 1924.)

I did this by gradually putting a rabbit closer to Peter each time he ate, until he was able to touch the rabbit without fear.
I must admit, I'm not as afraid of the boy as I used to be...

"Peter" was the first documented case of behaviour therapy (**Desensitization**) many years before it became popular!

Watson believed that by conditioning reflexes, i.e. controlling emotions, and by shaping behaviour in general, a better society could be constructed. (Watson, 1930.)

"For the universe will change if you bring up your children ... in behaviouristic freedom... Will not these children in turn, with their better ways of living and thinking, replace us as society and in turn bring up their children in a still more scientific way, until the world finally becomes a place fit for human habitation?"

Watson's Behaviourism was developed in the 1930s and 40s by several key figures: Tolman, Guthrie, Hull and – most famously – Skinner.

Skinner's Behaviourism

When **Burrhus Frederick Skinner** (1904-1990) published his first major book, *The Behaviour of Organisms* (1938), he sold few copies. But much more successful was *Science and Human Behaviour* (1953)...

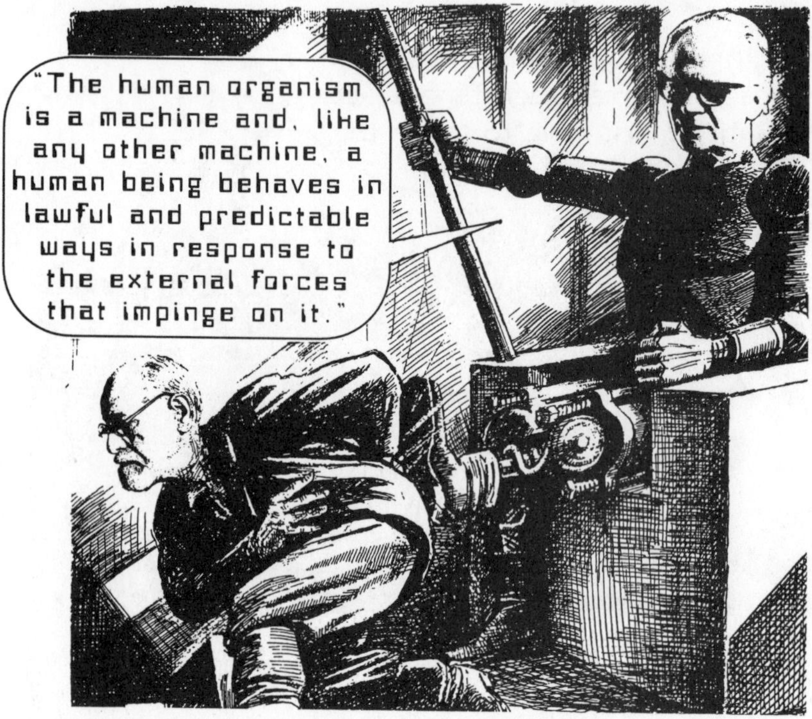

"The human organism is a machine and, like any other machine, a human being behaves in lawful and predictable ways in response to the external forces that impinge on it."

In contrast to Pavlov, who studied the Classical Conditioning of reflexes, Skinner studied mainly non-reflexive or **voluntary behaviour**.

Comparison of Pavlov and Skinner	
Pavlov's Classical Conditioning:	Skinner's Operant Conditioning:
Observable Stimulus → Response (reflex)	No observable Stimulus → Response (non-reflex)
animal responds – but can't change the environment i.e. **Respondent Behaviour**	animal operates on the environment i.e. **Operant Behaviour**

Operant Conditioning

Skinner invented an "Operant Conditioning Apparatus" (nicknamed the "Skinner Box" by Hull, 1933). The experiment: a hungry rat is placed in the box. Sooner or later, it accidentally presses the lever.

1. At first, no food pellets are released (to establish a baseline reading – Control Condition).

2. Then the food dispenser is connected.

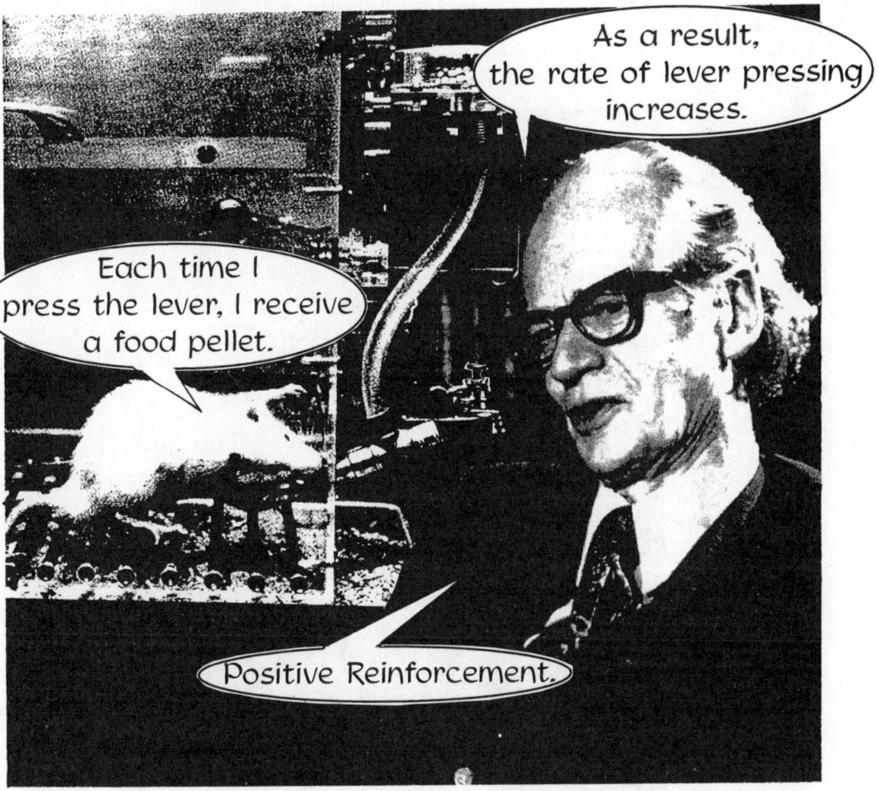

3. Next the food dispenser is disconnected. BUT the lever pressing still continues for some time. The rat has been **Operantly Conditioned**.

4. The lever pressing will actually continue indefinitely if occasional pellets are given – if **Partial Reinforcement** is given. Skinner researched different types of Partial Reinforcement, to see which was the most effective.

Partial Reinforcement Schedules

Skinner studied 4 types of situation. A pellet given:

1. Fixed Interval (FI) – e.g. once every minute

2. Variable Interval (VI) – e.g. after various intervals, averaging once a minute

3. Fixed Ratio (FR) – e.g. every 20 presses

4. Variable Ratio (VR) – e.g. after varying numbers of presses, averaging 20

Variable Ratio is "strongest" – responses continue longest before extinction, e.g. some pigeons responded thousands of times without reinforcement.

Time between response and reinforcement

Skinner found that the optimum period between response and reinforcement is about half a second, i.e. **almost immediately**. This is very important. For example, if a parent wants to reward or punish a child, then to be effective it should be done straight away.

This also explains one reason why the penal system often doesn't work. For instance, a burglar steals from a house. Three months later... the police arrest him. One year later... he is convicted in court. This is far too slow! But, according to Skinner, this isn't the only reason why punishment doesn't always work.

Why Punishment is Often Ineffective

1. In general, punishment is simply less effective because it causes SLOWER and LESS learned responses. It's better to use a combination of reward (Positive Reinforcement) and withdrawal of reward (Non-Reinforcement).

2. Punishment often causes the individual to AVOID BEING PUNISHED rather than stop the undesired behaviour...

3. Punishment can cause the individual to associate the punishment with the PUNISHER, rather than the BEHAVIOUR.

4. Punishment may train an individual about what NOT to do, but it doesn't train WHAT to do.

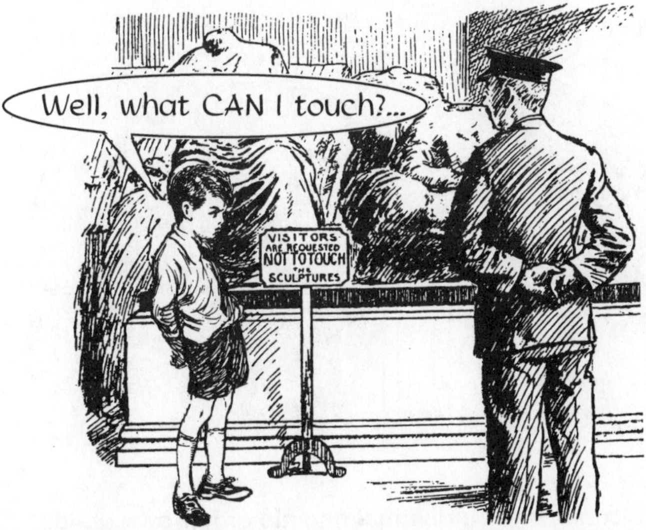

Skinner also found that many people (parents, teachers, judges...) make false assumptions about what is reward or punishment.

What is "Reward and Punishment"?

Skinner found that so-called "rewards" can have the opposite effect.

Similarly, so-called "punishment" can have the opposite effect.

According to Skinner, **each individual has his or her own needs.** Therefore, which reinforcement will "work", or not, must be found by experimenting with that particular animal or person.

Definitions ~ Putting it Into Practice

Before doing so, however, it's necessary to define the terms Positive and Negative Reinforcement, and Punishment. Since many people were so sloppy about words like "reward" and "punishment", Skinner defined the terms:

Positive Reinforcement is when there's an increase in behaviour by receiving anything that is pleasant (for example, food pellets for hungry rat).

Negative Reinforcement is when there's an increase in behaviour by avoiding something unpleasant (for example, rat pressing lever to avoid mild electric shock).

Punishment is when there's a decrease in behaviour by anything that is unpleasant.

"Problem Children"

Skinner realized that a lot of so-called "Problem" or "Naughty" children were really just normal, healthy, active children who had frequently been inadvertently "mis-trained" by their parents, teachers, etc. For example, the tendency to give attention (Positive Reinforcement) only when the child is "naughty", while ignoring the child when it is "good".

Even if the child is always "good" (which often just means "quiet and inactive", i.e. not necessarily healthy), then it may grow up to be neurotic – scared to do anything...

The 3-Stage Training Method

Ideally, said Skinner, all children should be trained correctly in the first place. (This is what successful parents naturally do, whether or not they're aware of it.) He devised a simple system: the **3-Stage Method** which he found to be effective on both animals and humans.

1. Define the Goal ("Terminal Behaviour")

Getting the dog to bark when it sees someone at the window...

2. Define the Start ("Entering Behaviour")

When it barks, then give it a treat! "You're a GOOD dog!" "Well done!"

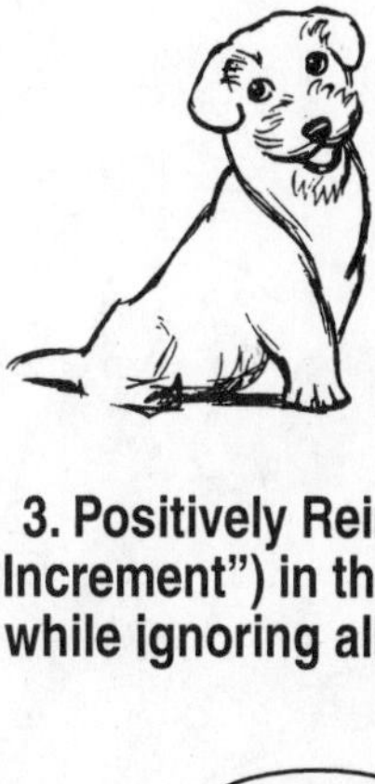

3. Positively Reinforce each step ("Increment") in the desired direction, while ignoring all other behaviour.

This is used, for example, to train guard dogs, police dogs and guide dogs for the blind. Based on this simple and effective approach, Skinner devised a method for changing behaviour.

Behaviour Modification

Skinner argued that some children and adults need to have their behaviour **modified** to fit into society and lead happier, more fulfilled lives. With children, it's usually a matter of changing the parents' behaviour as much as the child's. The Psychologist typically begins by helping the parents decide specifically what types of behaviour are desirable (Stage 1) and what are not (Stage 2).

DESIRABLE	NOT DESIRABLE
eating with utensils	throwing food
asking politely	screaming "I want..."
not swearing	swearing
sitting on chair	standing on chair
walking in corridor	running in corridor
etc.	etc.

Next, we have to decide on Stage 3. What Positive Reinforcement to give, what to ignore, and, if necessary, what Punishment.
Positive Reinforcements – praise, attention, treats...
Punishment – standing quietly for one minute in the hallway – "Time Out".

The key words are **consistency** – always reinforcing particular behaviour in the same way – and **firmness** – sticking to the programme.

Behaviour Modification is also used with some mentally ill patients in hospital. (Including "Token Economy", where plastic tokens are given which can be exchanged for rewards and privileges.)

Skinner's Contribution to Education

Skinner's "Three-Stage Method" has been applied not just to training but to education generally. Teachers decide what they want each child to achieve. They write down **Behavioural Objectives.**

> Example: "By the end of this book, you will be able to...
> – **state** a simple definition of Psychology
> – **describe** 3 types of work done by Psychologists
> – **contrast** Psychology with Psychiatry and Sociology
> – **list** at least 7 famous Psychologists... etc."
> NB The verbs must be **measurable**: nothing vague like "understand", "know", "grasp", "comprehend"...

Stating "objectives" is also a useful exercise for individuals deciding on their own study – or indeed ANY life goals they want to achieve!

> **TASK:** On a blank sheet of paper, write exactly what you want to achieve over the next 5 years. Don't be vague. Don't just write "rich", "successful"... Instead, write "achieving a capital of ________", or "successful at ________________________".

Society can change for the better (as depicted in Skinner's Utopian novel, *Walden Two*, 1948). It's up to us all to develop good HABITS (echoing William James) and improve Society through Conditioning.

However, Skinner wasn't the last word in Behaviourism. A "softer" approach developed taking into account behaviour that occurs without any obvious reinforcement.

Social Learning Theory

Not everyone agreed with Watson and Skinner's Radical Behaviourism – that all behaviour can be explained by Stimulus, Response and Reinforcement. It's also important to consider mental (cognitive) processes.

Julian Rotter (b. 1916) invented the term **Social Learning Theory** (1947) when studying social interactions in laboratory conditions. For him, humans have EXPECTATIONS about the effects of their behaviour, the kind of reinforcement they get, etc. In addition, people have their individual VALUES that they apply to their behaviour and the reinforcements they receive. An important question for Rotter is: **Where is your Locus of Control?**

There are basically two types of people, depending on their upbringing...
WHICH TYPE ARE YOU?

1. **Internal Locus of Control** people believe that reinforcement depends on personal efforts – thinking they are in charge of their lives and acting accordingly. They are physically and mentally healthier and more socially skilled. Their parents are supportive, generous with praise, consistent with discipline, and non-authoritarian.

2. **External Locus of Control** people believe that reinforcement depends on outside sources – so they make less attempts at improving their lives.

The Bobo Doll Experiments

Albert Bandura (b. 1925) developed a version of Behaviourism in the early 1960s, initially called "Sociobehaviorism" and then **Social Cognitive Theory**. Behaviour doesn't always have to be directly reinforced for it to occur. We can learn through simply **observing** others and seeing the consequences of their actions. This important "second-hand" learning is called "Vicarious Learning" or **Observational Learning**.

In the simplest experiment, Bandura (1963) used 2 groups of children.

The Experimental Group saw an adult in a room of toys being violent to an inflatable "Bobo" doll.
While the Control Group saw the adult playing non-violently...

Each child was then left alone in the toy-room and observed (on film)...

Bandura's Results

Without any direct encouragement, the Experimental Group performed significantly more aggressive acts than the Control Group.

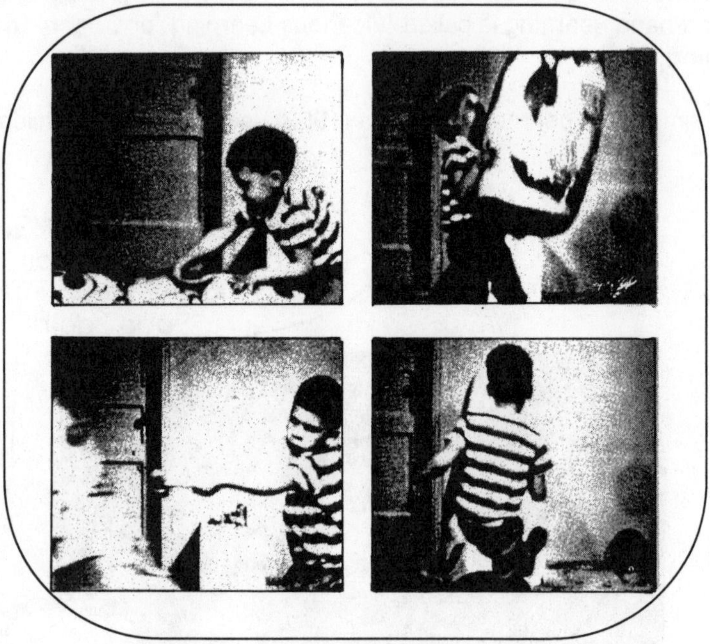

Conclusion: children will spontaneously IMITATE the behaviour of a MODEL, without any obvious reinforcement.

This was also an early demonstration that children will specifically imitate violence. Subsequent variations by Bandura – showing realistic and cartoon aggression on film – clearly showed that children can be strongly influenced by violence on TV and in the cinema. (Although these experiments didn't measure long-term effects.)

The processes of IMITATION and MODELLING have also been important in therapy.

"Modelling"

Like Skinner, Bandura applied his work to practical problems – modifying abnormal and undesirable behaviour. The therapist acts as a Model – showing a patient how to behave. For example, an arachnaphobic...

Modelling can be used to treat phobias, obsessive-compulsive disorders, sexual problems, anxieties, etc. **Education and Training** can also benefit: the teacher or trainer acts as a "Model" for the students.

Behaviourism, therefore, did eventually become less mechanistic, and more cognitive – sometimes called "Neo-Behaviourism". But this came too late to stop the early backlash against it.

3. THE COGNITIVE PERSPECTIVE

"Cognitive" basically means "Thinking" – perceiving, memory, language, problem-solving, and so on. The Cognitive Perspective is often seen as a contrast to the Radical Behaviourist view.

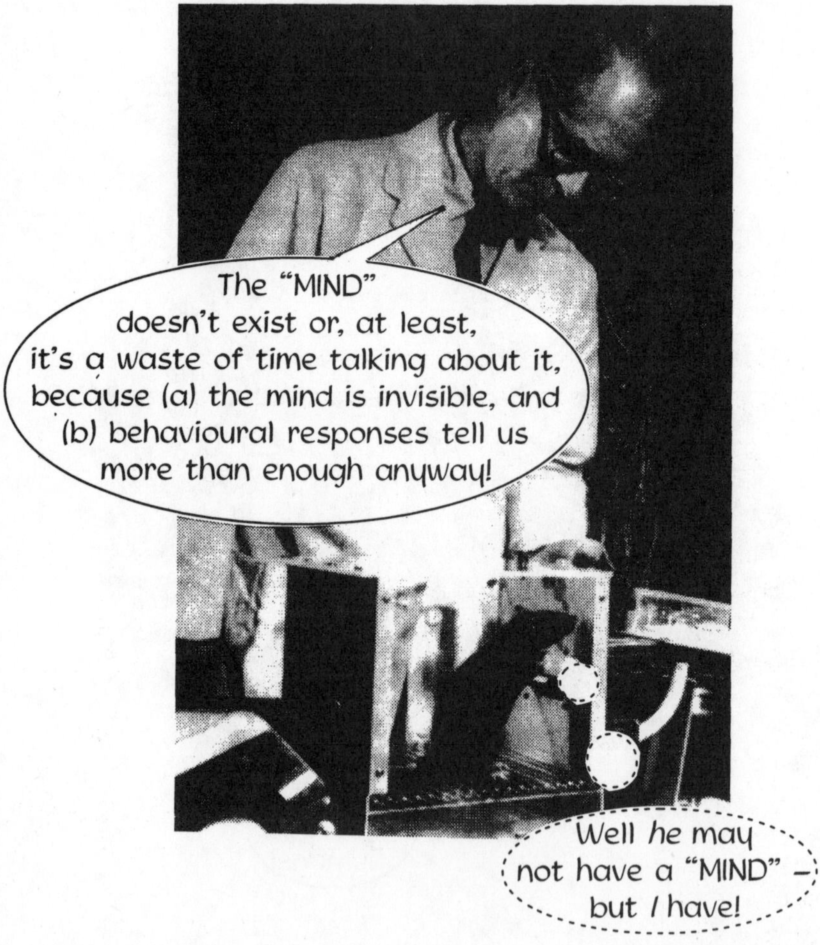

The "MIND" doesn't exist or, at least, it's a waste of time talking about it, because (a) the mind is invisible, and (b) behavioural responses tell us more than enough anyway!
Well *he* may not have a "MIND" – but *I* have!

In strict historical terms, the "true" Cognitive Movement didn't start until the late 1950s. However, ideas about the importance of mental processes and consciousness existed long before – in Structuralism and Functionalism, and especially in the Gestalt School. For this reason, the "Cognitive Perspective" here includes **Gestaltism** (even though they're often considered separately).

Gestalt Psychology

Although Psychology began in Germany, it developed in the USA through Structuralism, Functionalism and Behaviourism. But it was back in Germany that Behaviourism's major rival developed, at the same time, in **Gestaltism** – led by Wertheimer, Koffka and Köhler. (Although fate eventually also took them to the USA to escape the Nazis in the 1930s.) They particularly attacked the Wundtian approach of "elementism".

What does "Gestalt" mean?
There's no accurate translation of *Gestalt* (hence the original German word!) but, loosely, *Gestalt* means "form", "shape", "pattern"... with the emphasis being on "the whole".

The Active Mind

Gestalt Psychologists believe that the mind is ACTIVE and constantly looking for MEANINGS. They especially studied this in relation to visual perception, e.g. recognizing a human face.

In a strange place, we may look for a familiar face and may even briefly mistake a stranger for someone we know.
The roots of Gestaltism – especially the emphasis on the wholeness of perception – can be traced back to Kant.
"When we perceive... we encounter sensory elements that are meaningfully organized in an *a priori* fashion... thus, the mind creates a unitary experience."

The Gestaltists

Max Wertheimer (1880-1943) founded Gestalt Psychology when he published *Experimental Studies of the Perception of Movement* (1912). This article focussed on the illusion that there is apparent movement when a series of separate still images are seen rapidly. This is, of course, the basis for "films" or "movies" – at the rate of 28 frames per second. The central experiment was...

The Phi Phenomenon
Wertheimer made a simple set-up with two lights shining through two slits.

Wertheimer's simple demonstration is important for two reasons...

1. It contradicted Wundt:

Wertheimer's simple explanation was that apparent movement existed as it was perceived – it CANNOT be reduced further!

2. It's a neat demonstration of **the whole is greater than the sum of the parts**.

The Phi Phenomenon is, of course, also widely used today – in neon light advertising.

For his research, Wertheimer used two Ph.D. researchers...

Koffka and Köhler

Kurt Koffka (1886-1941) published the fundamental concepts of Gestalt Psychology in *Perception: An Introduction to Gestalt-Theorie* (1922). However, the title is misleading because Gestaltism is MUCH broader – including learning and thinking in general. Koffka's *Principles of Gestalt Psychology* (1935) is more definitive.

Wolfgang Köhler (1887-1967) was the main spokesman. He worked with Max Planck (founder of modern quantum physics), which strongly influenced his scientific approach. Köhler's most famous work was studying chimpanzees on Tenerife in the Canary Islands from 1913. The outbreak of World War I apparently stranded him there.

I worked for 7 years...
Documented in *The Mentality of Apes* (1927).

Returning to Germany, Köhler wrote another classic, *Static and Stationary Physical Gestalts* (1920) and the comprehensive *Gestalt Psychology* (1929).

Köhler's experiments provide us today with a fourth major learning theory (alongside Pavlov's Classical, Skinner's Operant, and Bandura's Social Learning Theories)...

Insight Learning Theory (or "Cognitive Learning")

Köhler set simple problem-solving tasks for the chimps. For instance, he left hollow bamboo sticks of different lengths and thickness outside the cage and a piece of fruit out of reach...

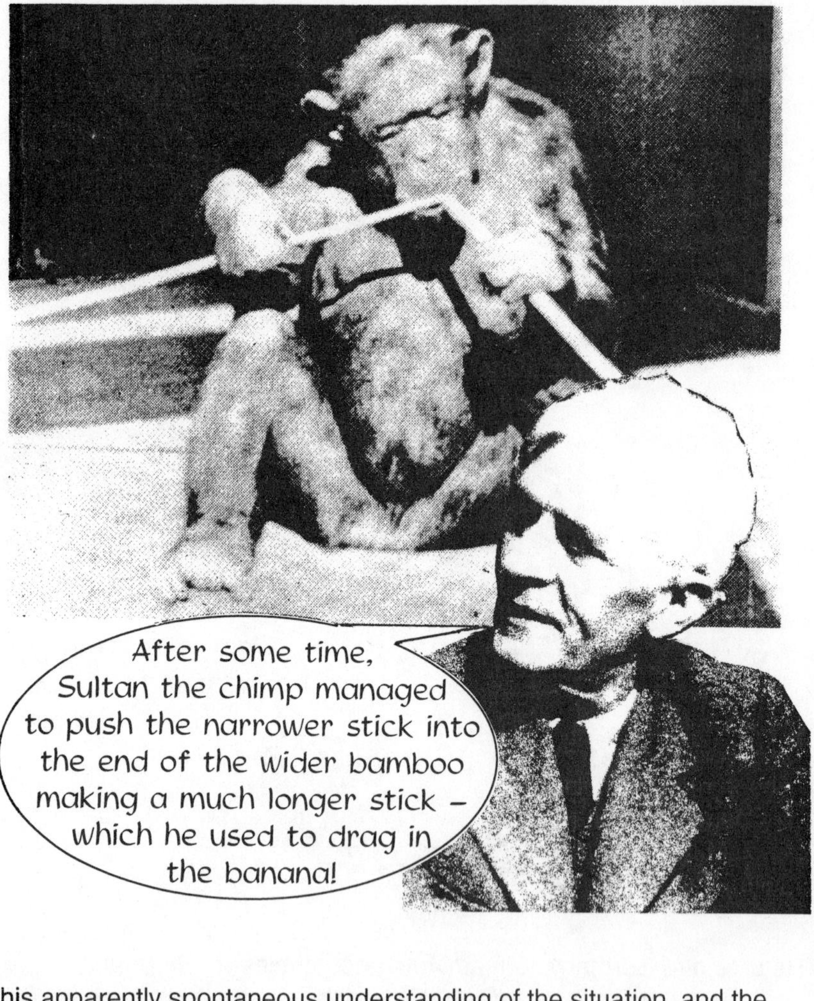

After some time, Sultan the chimp managed to push the narrower stick into the end of the wider bamboo making a much longer stick – which he used to drag in the banana!

This apparently spontaneous understanding of the situation, and the sudden solution, Köhler called **Insight** (*Einsicht*). It's also often called the "Ah-Ha!" phenomenon. As a Learning Theory, it's important because, unlike the other three, it takes into account the thought processes of the individual. People, and other animals, can learn by THINKING, not just by ("mindless") conditioning or imitation.

Gestalt Principles of Perception

Visual Perception, and that involving other senses, was carefully studied, especially by Wertheimer. Perception involves both the sense organs (e.g. seeing) and the brain (thinking).

Wertheimer believed that when we perceive an object, we experience the WHOLE effect or PATTERN – not just a collection of separate sensations. Here are some examples...

1. Proximity

o o o o o o o

– because the dots are close together, they are perceived together as a line. This is "The Law of Proximity".

2. Continuity

– we tend to perceive two lines crossing rather than two V-shapes.

3. Similarity

o x o x o x o
o x o x o x o
o x o x o x o
o x o x o x o

– vertical columns are perceived rather than horizontal rows.

4. Closure

– missing parts are assumed to be hidden or accidental.

5. Pragnanz (= "Goodness", "Simplicity"...) A sense of "goodness" or "rightness" is often experienced when objects are symmetrical, simple, stable...

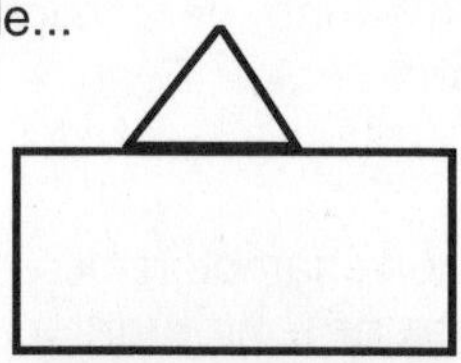

Good Pragnanz

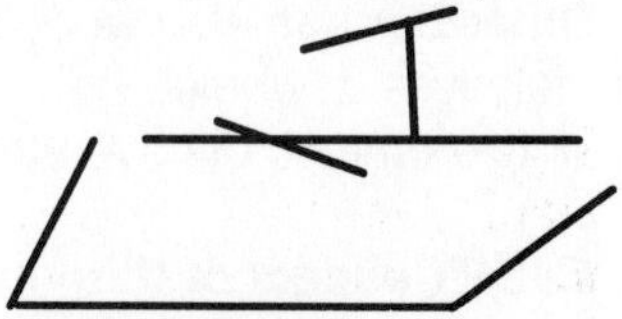

Bad Pragnanz

6. Figure/Ground Illusions

We tend to perceive some items in the foreground and others in the background. If the visual cues are AMBIGUOUS – it's not clear which is "front" or "back" – we "switch" from one view to another.

Rubin's Vase is usually equally perceived as a Vase or Two Faces.

Other Ambiguous Figures may be perceived in a certain way, depending upon the viewer's personality or expectations (**Mental Set**).

Illusions are simple demonstrations of the "active mind"...

Other Senses also work in this way. In auditory (hearing) perception, a melody is a "whole", not just a sequence of separate notes. Even simple tunes can have strong meanings!

EVERY aspect of thinking can have these Gestalt characteristics – emotional (e.g. being overwhelmed by a "whole event"), interpersonal, (e.g. the "whole character" of another person), social (e.g. the effect of a "whole group"), etc.

Applications of Gestalt

Therapy

A Gestalt Therapist will look at the "whole person" – not just the particular signs and symptoms of problems. A person's general life-style may be unsatisfactory: employment, domestic life, eating habits, exercise and activities, interests, etc. "Holistic Medicine" takes a similar approach.

Education

According to the Gestalt approach (see Wertheimer's *Productive Thinking*, 1945), the learner perceives the learning situation as a whole.

In addition, the teacher should...
1. provide activities that will stimulate
2. focus on general principles of problem-solving, rather than getting bogged down in petty details
3. encourage creativity, rather than mechanical repetition
So, the teacher should present the learning situation as a whole by providing overviews or outlines (the "Whole Picture") and summaries.

Field Theory

Kurt Lewin (1890-1947) extended Gestaltism to include human needs, personality, social influences – and especially motivation. Following Köhler's lead, and influenced by the pioneer quantum physicist Max Planck (1858-1947), he used the **Field Theory** of physics as a parallel for human situations.

Physicists after the 19th century thought less about the individual components of matter, (atoms, etc.) and more in terms of "Fields of Force" – regions or spaces affected by forces, such as magnetism, electricity, etc.

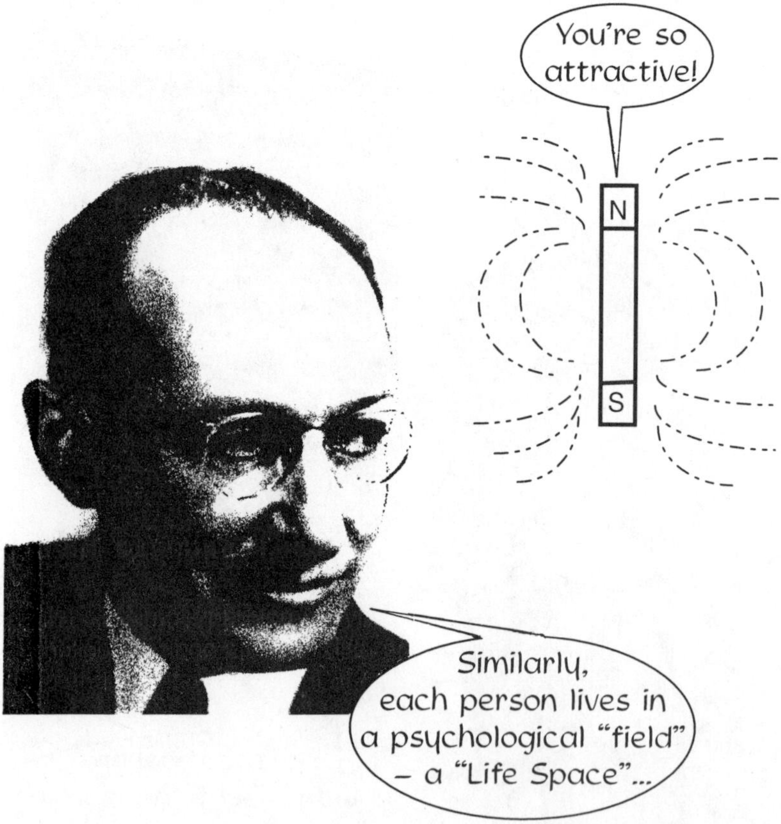

Lewin developed diagrams illustrating the past, present and future of lives or situations – including movement, barriers, outside influences, relationships, personal ambitions, etc. These help understanding, especially attempts at achieving **Equilibrium** between individuals and their environments.

Life-Space of a "Boy Who Wants to be a Doctor" (Lewin, 1936)

P = Boy as a Person
ce = college entrance exam
c = college
m = medical school
i = internship (assistant)
pr = starting own practice
G = Goal, i.e. Doctor

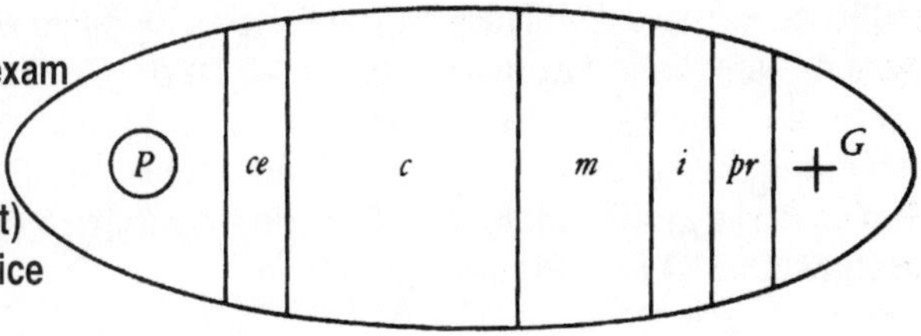

As well as individual behaviour, Lewin applied his concepts to group behaviour: Social Fields include sub-groups, lines of communication, barriers, goals, etc.

Lewin also provided us with a classic study on 3 "Styles of Leadership" in boys' groups: Authoritarian, Democratic and Laissez-Faire (Lewin, Lippitt, and White, 1939).

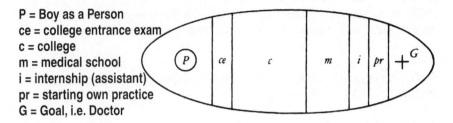

Today, Lewin's findings are applied in education, therapy (e.g. group therapies) and management.

The Cognitive Movement

Cognitive Psychology, as it's understood today, didn't really get going until Bruner and Miller established the "Center for Cognitive Studies" in 1960 at Harvard and Neisser published *Cognitive Psychology* (1967) which "established and christened the field" (Goleman, 1983).

The long background to this included not just the Gestalt Psychologists but other key individuals, e.g. Guthrie and Tolman (and other dissident Behaviourists) and Piaget (see later).

George Miller (b. 1920) was anti-Behaviourist.

I wanted a return to "common-sense" where the mind as well as behaviour could be studied. In practice, this meant researching perception, concept formation, memory, language, etc.
"It was supposed that no psychological phenomenon was real unless you could demonstrate it in a rat."

Ulric Neisser (b. 1928) also opposed the Radical Behaviourist approach.

After the publication of his 1967 book, Neisser became "The Father of Cognitive Psychology". He defined COGNITION as the processes "by which the sensory input is transformed, reduced, elaborated, stored, recovered, and used... cognition is involved in everything a human being might possibly do".

The advances in computing at that time had a considerable impact on Cognitive Psychology, in two important ways:

(a) The "Computer Model"

The mind is seen as a sort of computer...

HARDWARE = BRAIN **SOFTWARE = THOUGHTS (LANGUAGES)**

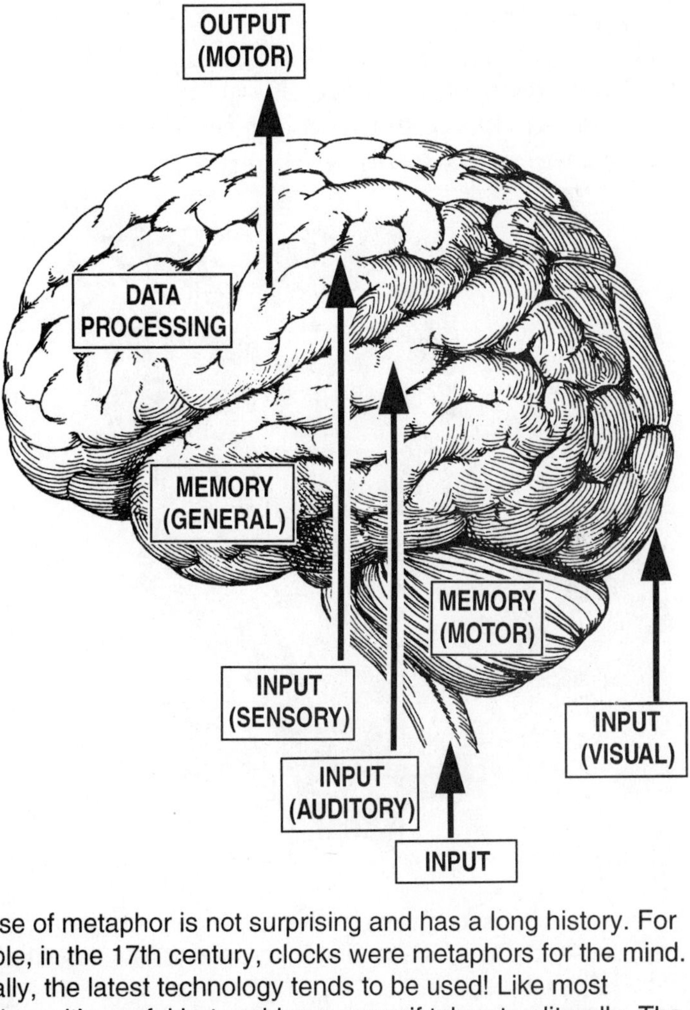

This use of metaphor is not surprising and has a long history. For example, in the 17th century, clocks were metaphors for the mind. Basically, the latest technology tends to be used! Like most metaphors, it's useful but problems occur if taken too literally. The fact remains that even the world's largest computer is still extremely limited compared to any human brain!

(b) Research using computers

The ability to collect, collate and analyze data using computers has helped the whole of Psychology. But there's been (arguably) a tendency in Cognitive Psychology to overuse the computer as a research tool: laboratories are frequently used to test individuals using computer programmes.

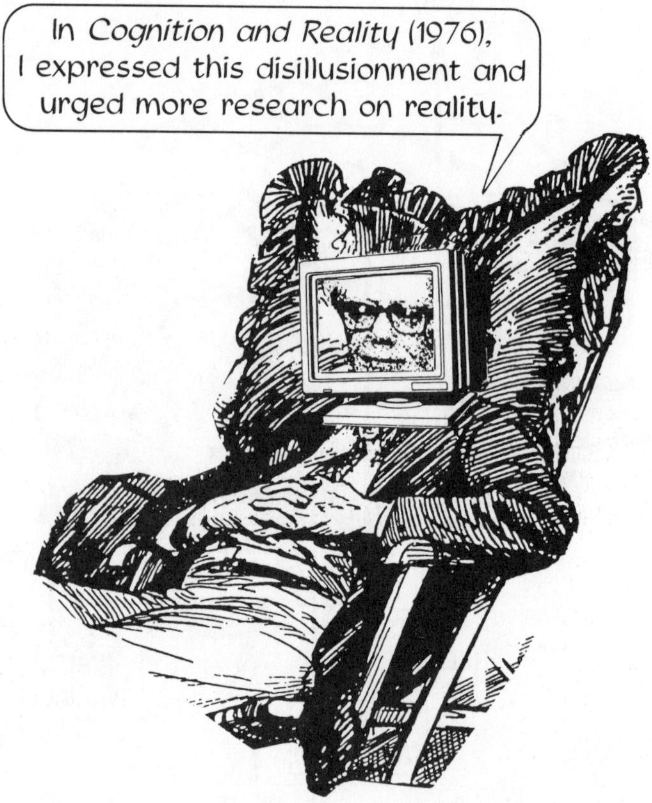

In *Cognition and Reality* (1976), I expressed this disillusionment and urged more research on reality.

Despite these problems, cognitive factors are widely considered in current applications – in educational, clinical, social, industrial and organizational psychology.

But the emphasis on human beings as individuals has an approach of its own.

4. THE HUMANISTIC PERSPECTIVE

Humanistic Psychology also developed in the 1960s (like the Cognitive movement) and was known in America as "The Third Force", after Psychoanalysis and Behaviourism.

Main Humanistic Ideas

1. Focus on the INDIVIDUAL, especially personal choice: free will, creativity, spontaneity.

2. Emphasis on CONSCIOUS experience.

3. Everything to do with the wholeness of HUMAN NATURE.

It's possible to trace various roots: William James, Gestaltists, certain post-Freudians (Adler, Jung, Horney, Erikson, Allport).

Humanistic Psychology also developed out of PHENOMENOLOGY – the study of immediate experience as it occurs (Muller, Stumpf, Husserl) – a precursor to Gestalt Psychology.

But that's too difficult for many people to say!
Krazy Dazies are
PRODUCTIONS
LOVE
The Humanistic approach can be seen as being part of a broader Phenomenological Perspective.

But, whatever the past, the *Zeitgeist* of the 1960s provided the perfect environment for this flower to blossom.

The Philosophy of Humanistic Psychology

The Humanistic Psychologists, more than anyone, saw Behaviourism as being very narrow – reducing humans to the level of programmable machines.

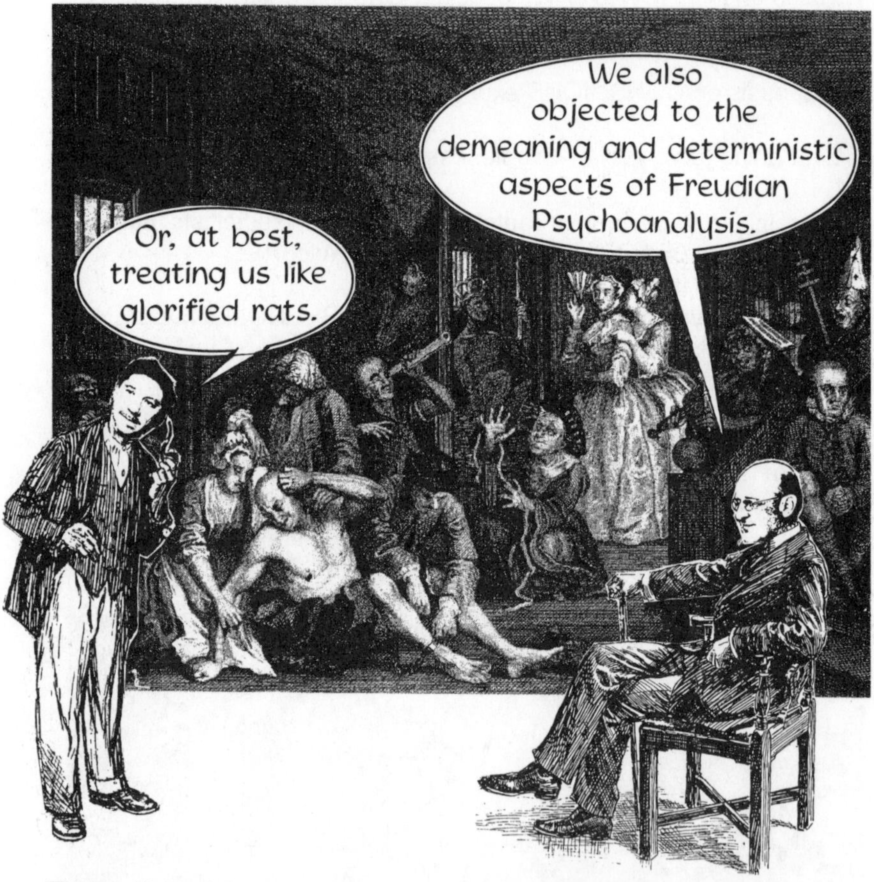

They criticized the Freudian emphasis on mental illness – and all the negative aspects of human nature – misery, jealousy, hatred, fear, selfishness.

Instead, the Humanists wanted to concentrate on Mental Health, with all the positive attributes of happiness, contentment, ecstasy, kindness, caring, sharing, generosity, and so on.

Two men in particular shared this vision, Maslow and Rogers...

Maslow

Abraham Maslow (1908-70) was the "Spiritual Father" of Humanistic Psychology. He started out an enthusiastic Behaviourist, but became very unhappy about the limitations of that approach – especially that it seemed to ignore "real people".

Maslow had been inspired by two particular individuals he knew, both teachers of his – Ruth Benedict (Anthropologist) and Max Wertheimer (Gestalt Psychologist).

The result of this research (in *Motivation and Personality*, 1970, and *The Farther Reaches of Human Nature*, 1971), was the theory of SELF-ACTUALIZATION: the innate human motivation, that each of us has, to ACHIEVE OUR POTENTIAL by using and developing our talents and abilities. Each time we experience such a sense of fulfillment is called a PEAK EXPERIENCE.

In order to reach Self-Actualization, we have to satisfy lower "needs" that exist at different levels.

The Hierarchy of Needs

Each Need must be satisfied before the next Need up can motivate us.

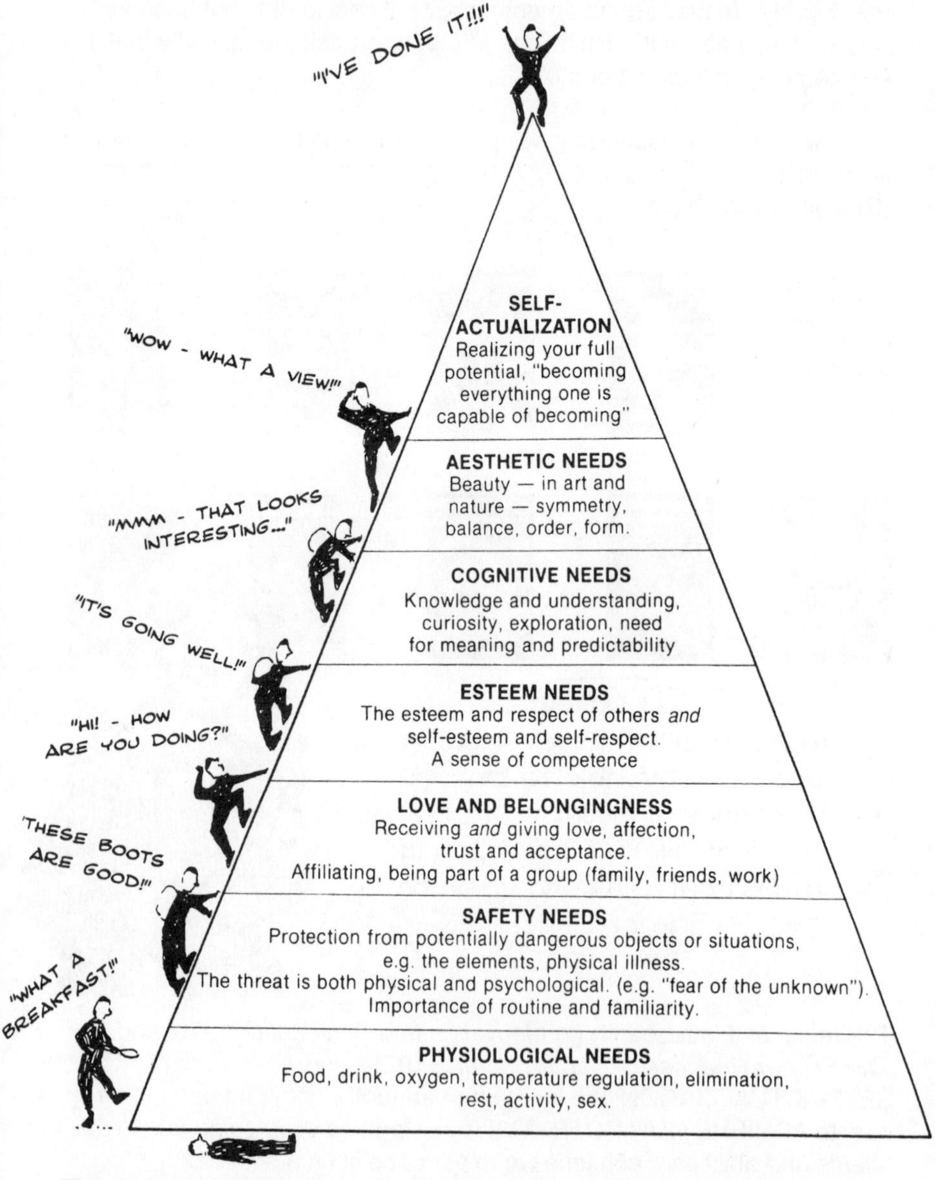

This is like a ladder where, starting from the bottom, each Need must be satisfied before the next Need up can motivate us. Everyday each of us may go up and down the hierarchy several times, reaching different levels before returning to the bottom again.

Application of The Hierarchy

Education: training teachers to motivate students; helping students plan their own study (setting goals, having regular breaks).

Therapy: helping patients understand their own needs and those of others (the need for love and affection, the importance of self-esteem).

Management: training managers to understand the needs of staff and help motivate them (the need for good washroom and canteen facilities, the need for praise and encouragement, and so on).

So, what ARE those characteristics that Maslow found?

Psychologically "healthy" people show

1. An objective perception of reality
2. Acceptance of their own natures
3. A commitment and dedication to some type of work
4. Naturalness, simplicity in behaviour, and spontaneity
5. Independence; a need for autonomy and privacy
6. Intense mystical / peak experiences
7. Empathy with, and affection for, all humanity – including strong social interests
8. Resistance to conformity
9. Democratic characteristics
10. Keenness to be creative

Incidentally, Maslow also found that only about 1% of the population are Self-Actualizers, and they are typically middle-aged or older and free from neuroses!

BUT – ANYONE can have Peak Experiences if they work at it! Which is one thing that Rogers tried to help people to achieve.

Rogers

Carl Rogers (1902-87) developed a theory of Self Actualization that is very similar to Maslow's. It also emphasizes an innate drive towards achieving one's potential. However, there are subtle differences: Rogers prefers to see the process as being ongoing – hence, his preference for the term **Self Actualizing**, rather than Maslow's **Self Actualization**.

Also, Rogers thought that childhood upbringing, especially the role of the mother, was a crucial factor in adult personality.

A healthy personality derives from the mother's unconditional love – "Positive Regard" – as opposed to "Conditional Positive Regard" which limits the development of the self.

To Rogers (1961), the psychologically healthy person has:
1. An openness to all experience
2. An ability to live fully in every moment
3. The will to follow their own instincts, rather than the will of others
4. Freedom in thought and action, e.g. spontaneity, flexibility
5. Much creativity

Rogerian Therapy

Rogers developed a form of psychotherapy called **Person Centred Therapy** (or "Client Centred").

The essence of PCT is that the Client (not "patient") is responsible for improving his or her life. This was a deliberate change from both the Psychoanalytic and the Behaviourist approaches – and conventional medicine in general – where patients are "diagnosed" by a "doctor" (or other "expert") and GIVEN "treatment". In Rogerian Therapy, the therapist is not responsible for changes in the client.

The Self Concept

Rogers particularly emphasized the role of the **Self Concept**, which consists of three parts – **Ideal Self, Self Image** and **Self Esteem**.

Self Esteem depends on the gap between Ideal Self and Self Image...
Therefore, Self Esteem can be increased by raising the Self Image, lowering the Ideal Self, or both!

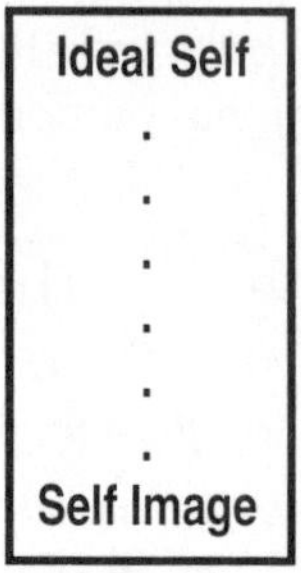
Ideal Self
Self Image

LARGE GAP = Low Self Esteem

Ideal Self
Self Image

SMALL GAP = High Self Esteem

Rogers' approach has had a major impact on psychotherapy and on "self improvement" for the general public. Unfortunately, many charlatans have tried to jump on the "human potential" bandwagon, over the years, doing more harm than good. Also, the Humanistic movement has still not become a "School" because there is no strong scientific theory or research to continue a tradition.

But then, neither can the next two Perspectives be called Schools...

5. THE BIO-PSYCHOLOGICAL PERSPECTIVE

Bio-Psychology (also called Biological or Physiological, or Neuro-Psychology) seeks to describe and explain behaviour in terms of **nerves** and **chemicals** in the body, especially the **brain**.

Bio-Psychology has existed from the beginning of Psychology, having developed from Physiology.
Bio-Psychology's progress is closely linked to the technological advances for observing and measuring the body – from early optical microscopes to recent scanning systems.

Although not a School, it has a strong tendency towards a **reductionist approach** – "reducing" behaviour to its neuronal and biochemical elements. To most Bio-Psychologists, the "mind" and "consciousness" are simply the activities of the brain. Some say (e.g. Hebb, Pribram) that Psychology is really a biological science.

A common interest in Bio-Psychology has been to find out what different parts of the brain do, known as **Localization of Function**.

The Geography of the Brain

To put it simply, the brain consists of **surface**, **interior** and **two hemispheres**. Let's look briefly at each in terms of identifying "local functions".

1. The **surface** or **cortex** (from the Latin "bark" because of its convoluted look) is about 80% of the brain. It has been "mapped", as far as this is appropriate.

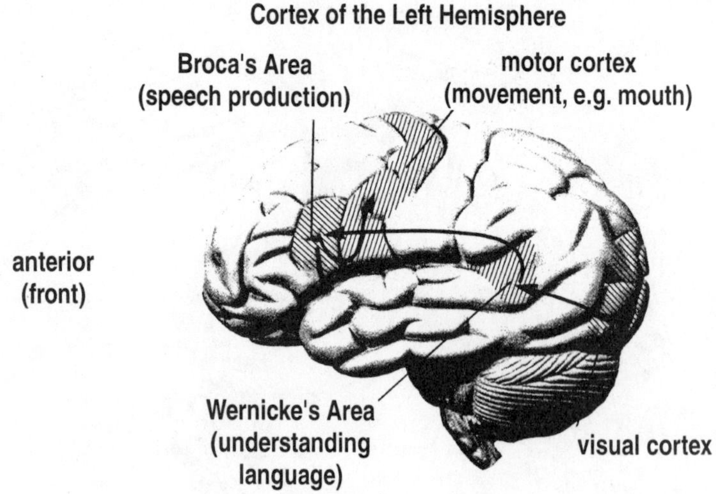

2. Here is an **interior** cross-section of the brain which features its basic functional structures.

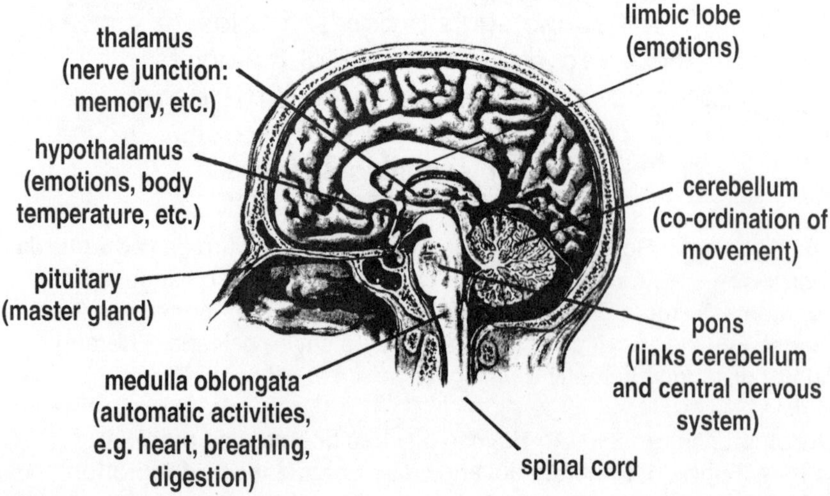

3. The brain is made up of two halves or **hemispheres** joined by a piece of tissue called the **corpus callosum**. In normal people, there appears to be some specialization in each hemisphere. In general, the left brain controls the right side of the body, while the right brain controls the left side.

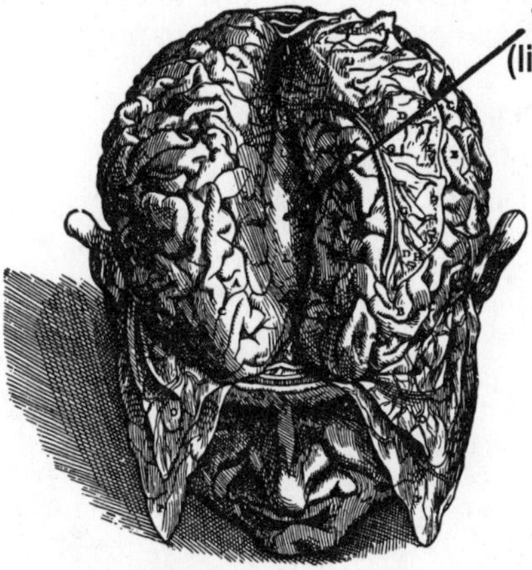

In addition, for most people, the left brain seems to specialize in language skills (e.g. understanding and producing speech) while the right deals with visual-spatial skills (e.g. drawing, perceiving patterns, using maps).

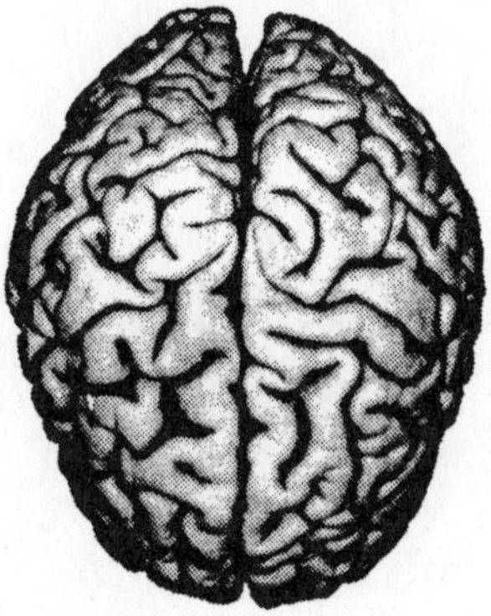

Some argue that we often neglect to use the right side enough (see Betty Edwards, *Drawing on the Right Side of the Brain*, 1979). There is also some evidence of gender differences. Linguistically, males show more left-hemisphere dominance; women show more bilateral, symmetrical patterns of function. (Kimura, 1987)

"Split Brain" Experiments

Roger Sperry (1964) found that the two hemispheres seem to work independently if the corpus callosum is cut. Sperry's experiments on animals were subsequently tried on humans with epilepsy – to try stopping their sudden damaging "brain storms" that travel from one side to the other. This seemed to help reduce the devastating effects of epileptic fits in such "Split Brain" patients. But sometimes they behaved bizarrely, as though possessing two separate minds.

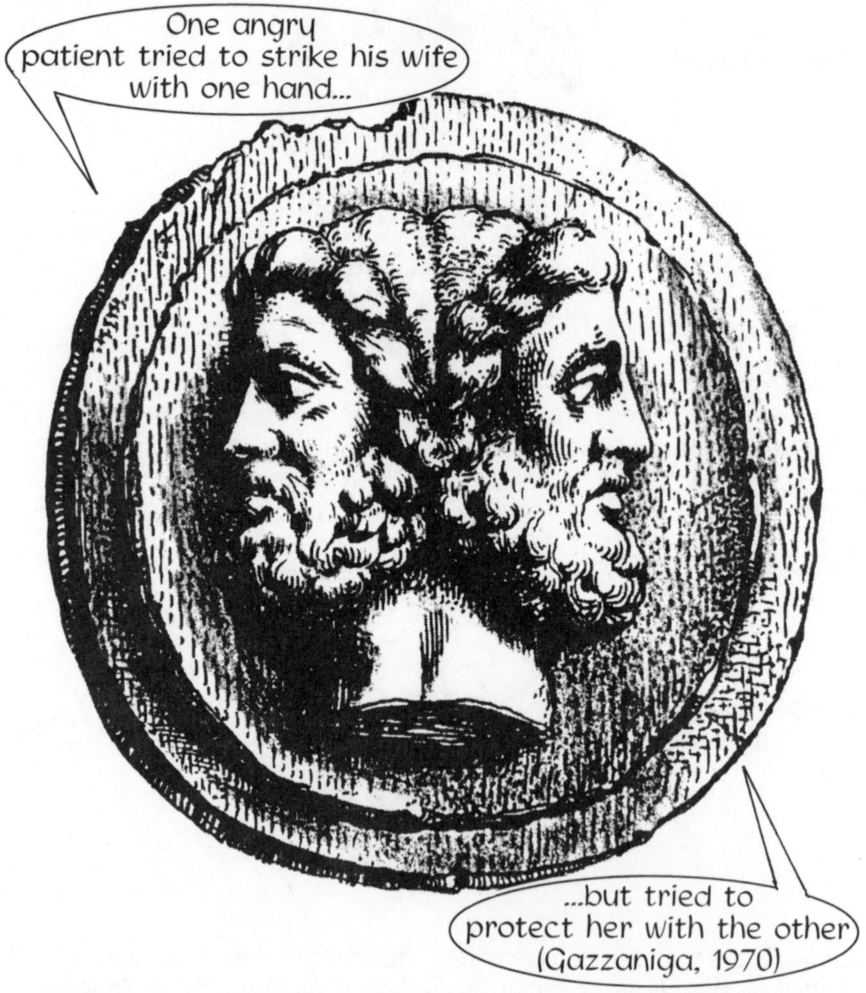
One angry patient tried to strike his wife with one hand...
...but tried to protect her with the other (Gazzaniga, 1970)

(By the way, this has nothing to do with "schizophrenia", which is often wrongly translated as "split personality" – a better description is "fractured personality". True "Multiple personalities" are extremely rare.)

Brain Research

Localization of Function seems to apply to some activities (e.g. sensory and motor functions) but it is wrong to take the concept too far! Much of the brain's activities involve many areas working together. Also, clinical case studies have demonstrated that although large areas of the brain can be damaged or missing, other parts can take over.

The brain can now be studied using several non-intrusive techniques. One well-established way of measuring brain activity is the EEG or "Electro-Encephalogram" (started by H. Berger, 1929). This can be used on a conscious person without discomfort.

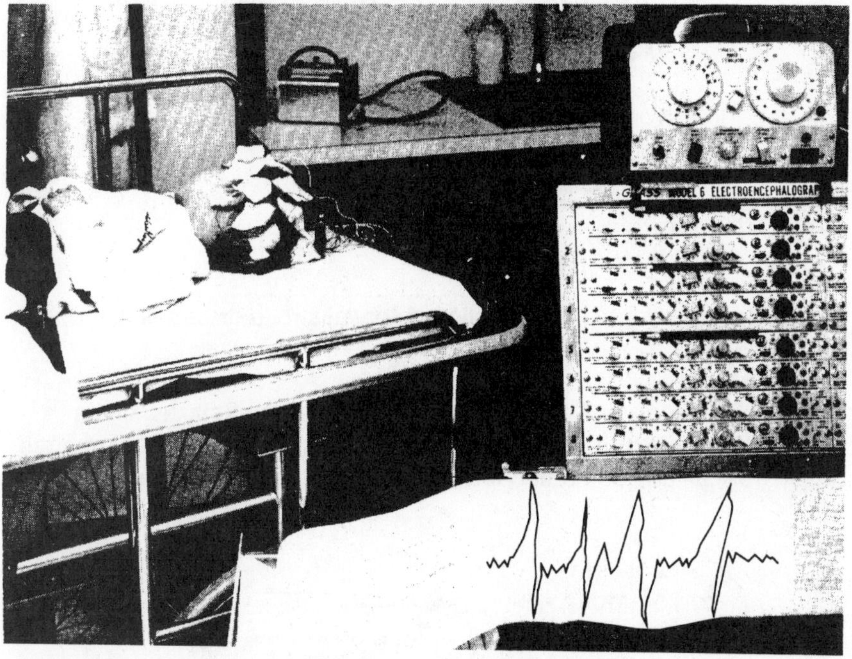

By attaching surface electrodes to the skin (hair does not need to be removed), the electrical activities of the cortex just under the skull can be picked up, amplified and seen on a meter or pen-plotter. This, for example, is a standard test to detect signs of epilepsy, which show as extreme spikes.

However, apart from obvious readouts (e.g. epilepsy, death), an EEG can be hard to "read"! But there are other non-intrusive techniques.

Other Brain Research Techniques

(a) The Angiogram is essentially an X-ray picture of dyes injected into the blood. It is therefore limited to blood vessels and activity.

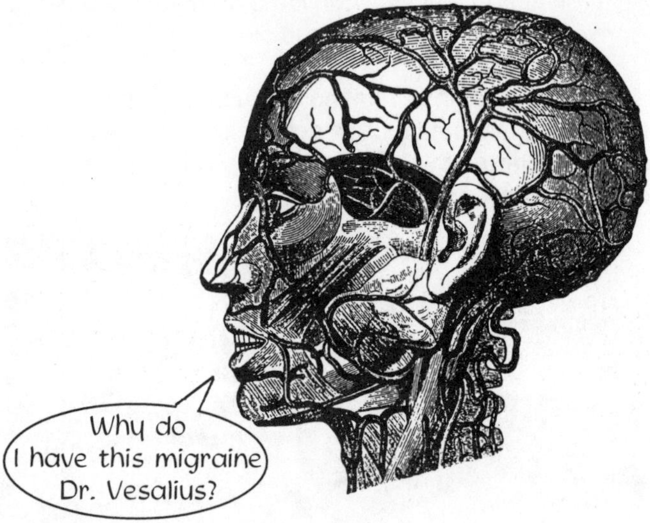

However, it is valuable for detecting potential stroke diseases, tumours, etc.

(b) The CAT scan or Computerized Axial Tomogram (started in the early 1970s) is a more sophisticated X-ray picture composed of images taken from all angles around the head using a doughnut-shaped ring.

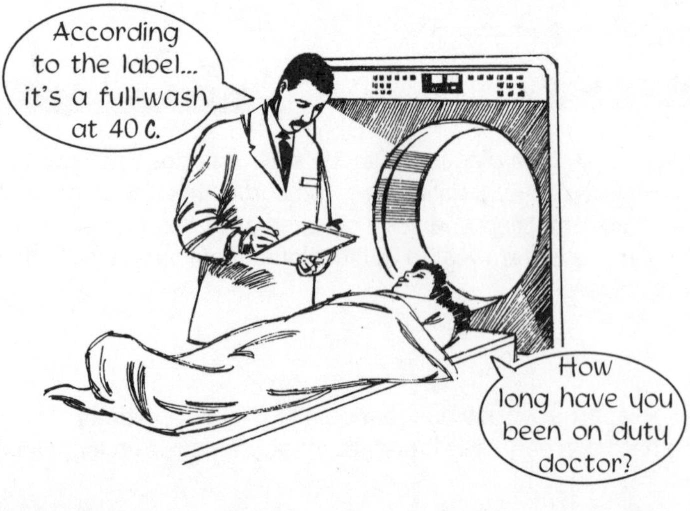

(c) PET or Positron Emission Tomography scan (from the 1980s), uses mildly radioactive glucose injected into the body and detectors to create MOVING pictures of the active brain. Thus, the brain can be seen working while someone is active – speaking, listening to music, drawing...

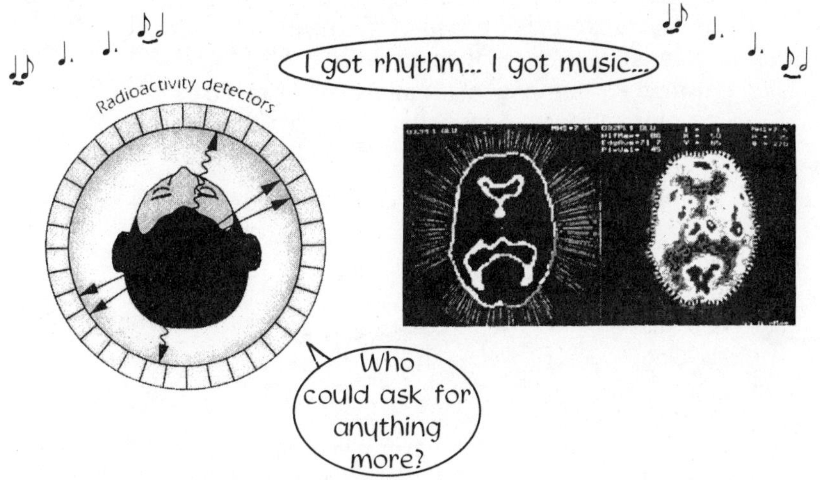

(d) MRI: Magnetic Resonance Imaging (Schulman, 1983) uses no radiation but radio-waves in a strong magnetic field – which moves in small (noisy) steps, as the person lies in a tube – to detect the effects on the molecules in the body.

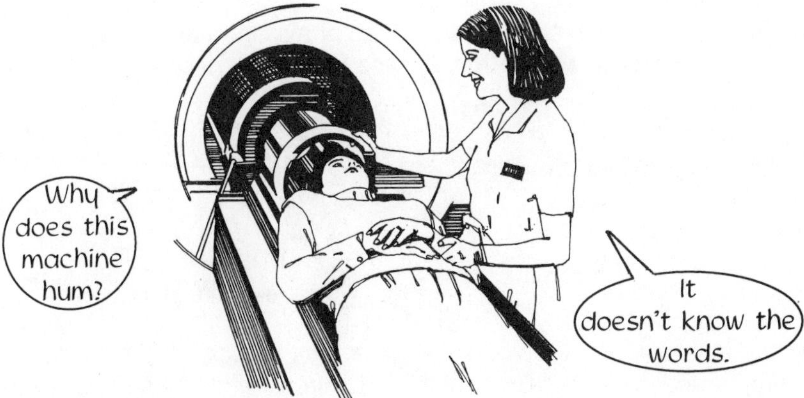

All these scans are hospital-based, time-consuming and expensive.

The Nervous System

This consists of nerve cells or **neurons** linked by **synapses**.

Neurons

The brain consists of about 15 billion neurons that can each be connected to hundreds of others.

> **There are three types of neuron:**
> sensory = receiving information
> motor = carrying information, e.g. to muscles
> interneurons = connections between the above

A typical neuron:

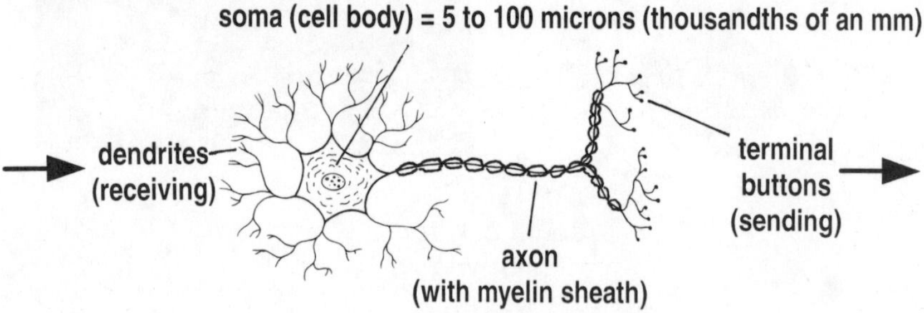

Donald Hebb (1949) produced the Cell Assembly Theory that particular actions or ideas are caused by sets of neurons linked together. When one neuron is active, it sends a message via the axon to the next neuron...

Synapses

At the end of each axon is a narrow gap or **synapse** across which chemicals, or **neurotransmitters**, pass to the next neuron...

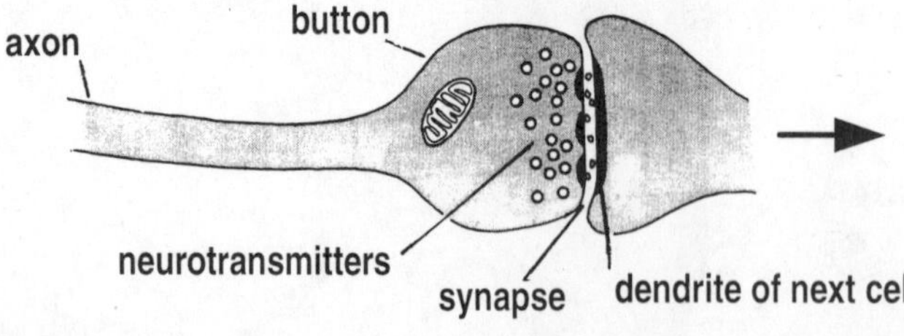

When a neuron activates ("fires") another in this way, it's like a switch being turned on – it is "all or nothing". Neurons "fire" like a line of falling dominoes. Of course, as well as "exciting" other neurons, it's necessary to sometimes "inhibit" them so that they DON'T become active. Thus, there are different types of neurotransmitters.

Neurotransmitters

Three very important chemicals are:

1. Acetylcholine (or ACh) excites and may be responsible for memory.

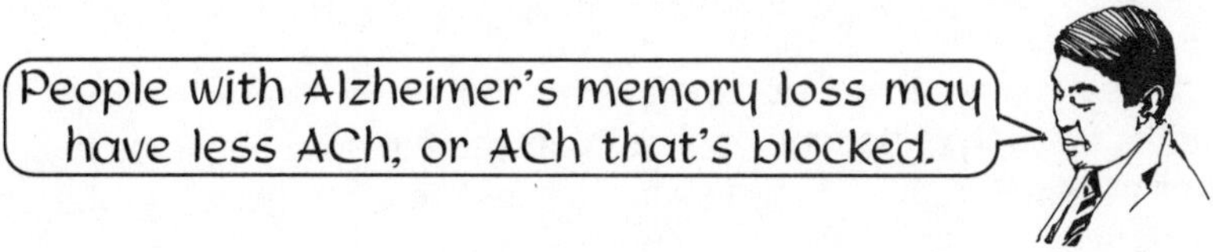

People with Alzheimer's memory loss may have less ACh, or ACh that's blocked.

2. Dopamine excites and is involved in movement, attention and learning.

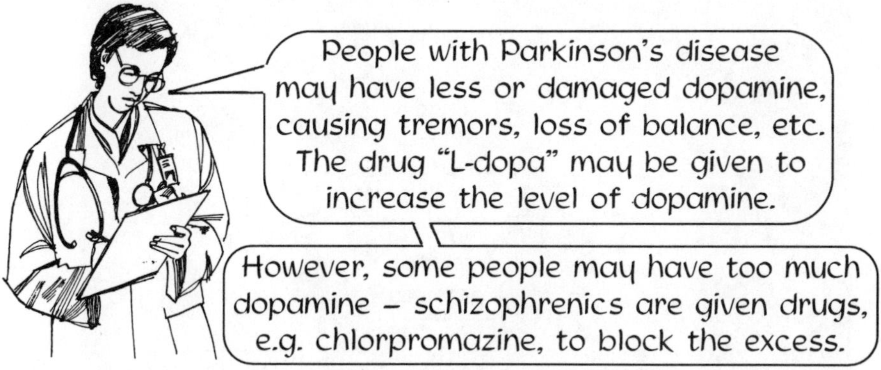

People with Parkinson's disease may have less or damaged dopamine, causing tremors, loss of balance, etc. The drug "L-dopa" may be given to increase the level of dopamine.
However, some people may have too much dopamine – schizophrenics are given drugs, e.g. chlorpromazine, to block the excess.

3. Serotonin (or 5-HT) usually inhibits and is involved in arousal and sleep (e.g. inhibiting dreaming), mood (e.g. inhibiting depression), appetite and sensitivity.

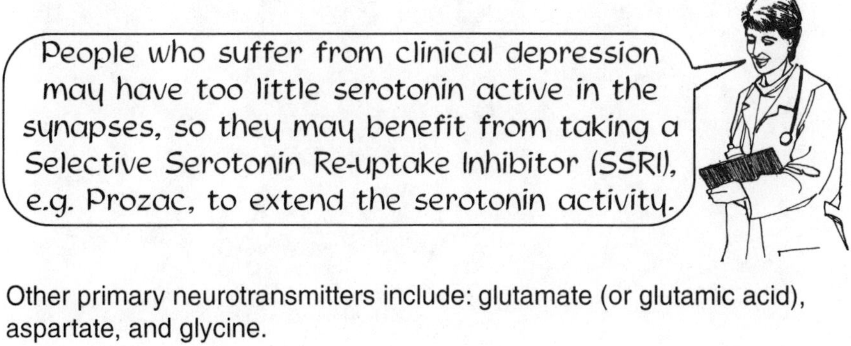

People who suffer from clinical depression may have too little serotonin active in the synapses, so they may benefit from taking a Selective Serotonin Re-uptake Inhibitor (SSRI), e.g. Prozac, to extend the serotonin activity.

Other primary neurotransmitters include: glutamate (or glutamic acid), aspartate, and glycine.

In addition to the Nervous System, there's another major form of communication system, as we'll now see.

The Endocrine System

The nervous system acts quickly (hundredths of a second) so that we can respond immediately to the environment. The endocrine system generally has a relatively slower (several seconds or minutes) and more long-term effect on behaviour.

This is because the endocrine system (meaning, "inside secretions") works through endocrine "glands" that secrete special chemicals – **hormones** – into the blood system, affecting other glands or the body generally.

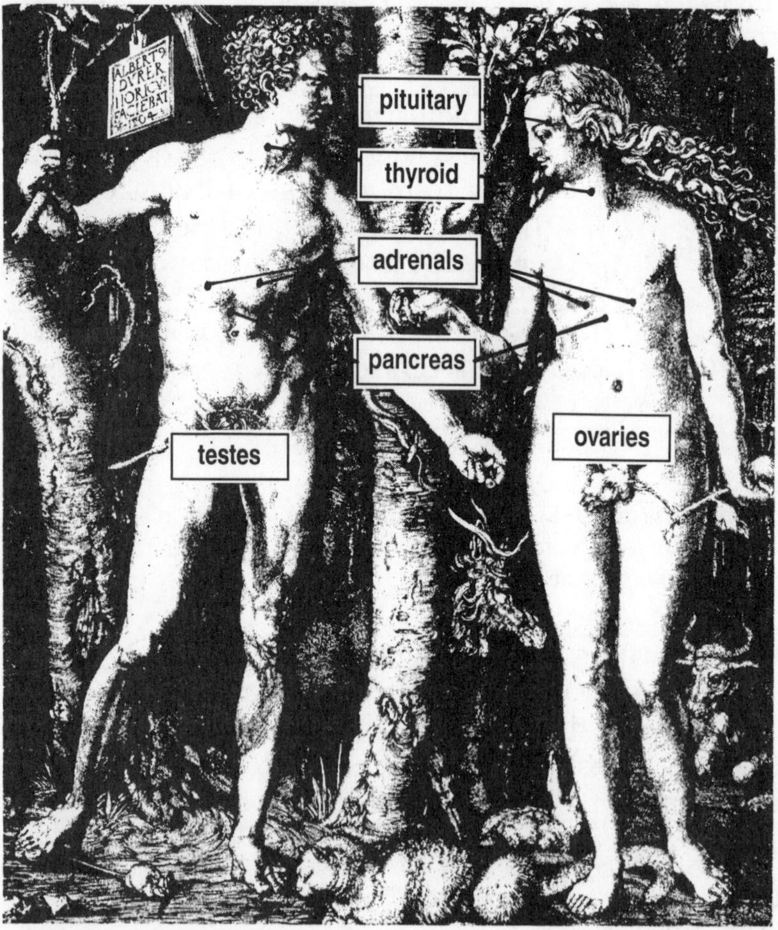

Psychologists are especially interested in the pituitary, adrenal, and gonads. The thyroid and pancreas are mainly involved in digestion (although abnormalities in those can cause mood changes).

The Glands

The Pituitary is known as "The Master Gland" because it controls the other glands.

For example, in a stressful situation, messages are received from the hypothalamus (the adjoining brain part which links the nervous and endocrine systems). Then the pituitary secretes ACTH ("Adrenocorticotropic Hormone") which is carried in the bloodstream to the adrenals (and other glands).

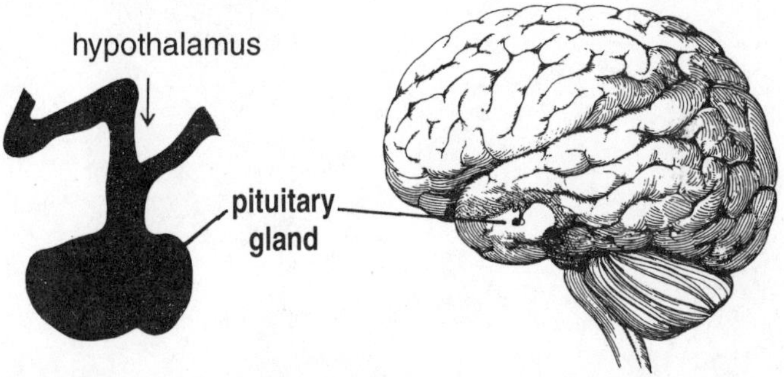

The Adrenals are important glands that cope with stress and with mood and energy levels. For example, when the ACTH is received (when under stress, as above), the inner core secretes adrenaline (or "epinephrine") that prepares the body for emergency, causing increased heart-beat, perspiration, and so on.

Other important activities involve the **sex glands**.

The Sex Glands

The testes produce "testosterone" which is an "anabolic steroid". "Anabolic" means "building up" – it builds muscle and breaks down fats. Testosterone is produced relatively constantly and is one cause of aggressive behaviour (Hutt, 1972).

Male aggression can be seen in most animals, including humans, at all ages. (Exceptions include pregnant females, mothers, and certain insects such as the praying mantis and Black Widow spider.)

Thus, testosterone has been seen as a possible innate cause of gender differences. For example, most violent crimes are committed by men. However, some psychologists believe that the "testosterone explanation" has been over-stated, emphasizing the **correlational** relationship of testosterone and aggression in some research (Maccoby and Jacklin, 1974).

The ovaries produce "oestrogens" (or "estrogens") and "progesterone".

Oestrogens are "catabolic steroids". "Catabolic" means "breaking down" – they break down muscle and build fat. (They also cause water retention, hence the weight increases at certain times of the month.)

Progesterone prepares the female for pregnancy ("gestation") – lining the uterus, lactation, stopping egg production.

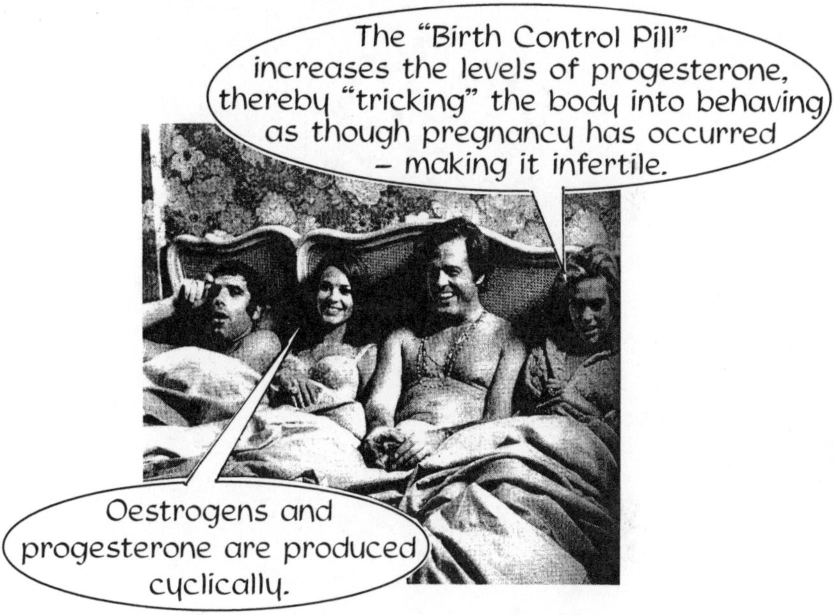

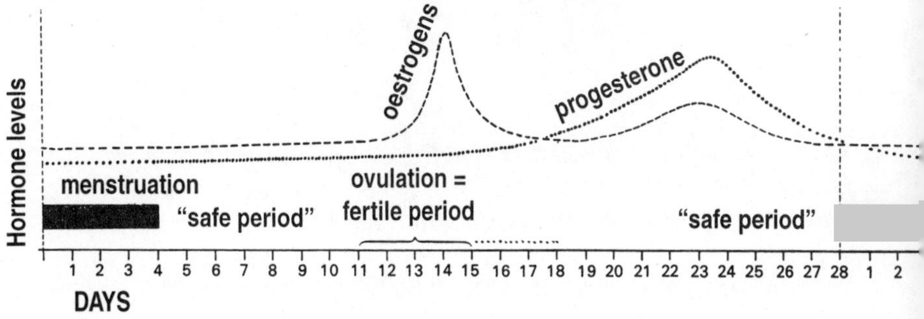

Summary:
Male hormones are CONSTANT and SIMPLE (like a glass of spirits!)
Female hormones are CYCLIC and COMPLEX (like a cocktail!)

Genetics

Each cell in a human being contains DNA ("Deoxyribonucleic Acid"), in which all the information is stored to make the whole body.

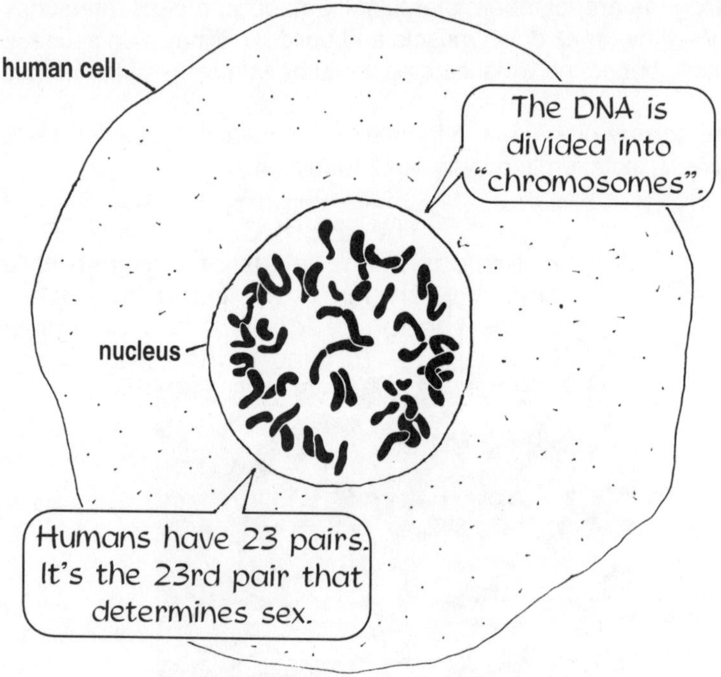
human cell
The DNA is divided into "chromosomes".
nucleus
Humans have 23 pairs. It's the 23rd pair that determines sex.

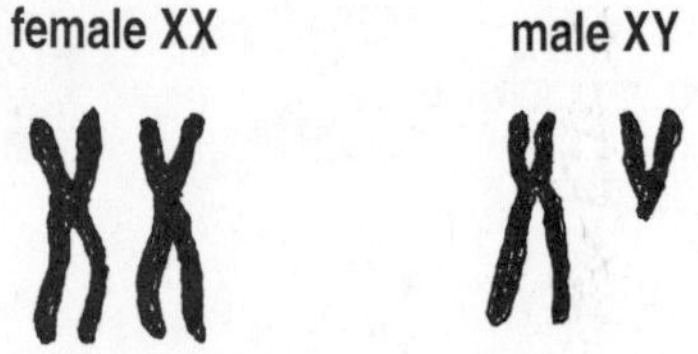
female XX
male XY

Each chromosome consists of hundreds of **genes** – the biological units that help determine characteristics – which are transferred from parents to offspring during sexual reproduction.

Each person's cell DNA has about 100,000 genes.

Currently, the "Genome Project" is pooling the international findings of biologists in order to map *every* human gene. This has medical applications in identifying genes that cause diseases, e.g. Duchenne's Muscular Dystrophy, Huntington's Chorea, etc.

Genetics in Psychology

While some individual genes do seem to have specific functions (a gene for brown or blue eye colouring), on the whole, genes seem to work together to produce physical characteristics.

Generally, though, genes don't seem to be directly responsible for particular behaviour.

There's unlikely to be a "criminal" or "gay" or "intelligence" gene – as claimed in recent years.
However, some argue that groups of genes may cause a predisposition to behave in such ways. The jury is still out.

Having said that, animal research has demonstrated that it *is* possible to breed for general behavioural characteristics – intelligence, affection, aggression, etc. So, in theory at least, it could apply to humans. But even if it does – what then? There are important ethical implications.

The "Big Debate" remains the "Nature vs Nurture" issue. To what extent does the genetic make-up or the environment determine behaviour? Today, "Interactionism" takes the view that both are vital and can't be separated.

A favourite research approach has been to study humans born with identical genes – twins...

Twin Studies

Using correlations, identical twins reared apart have been compared (for intelligence, schizophrenia, etc.) to try to determine the importance of genes.

Researchers in the USA and the UK found significant positive correlations (above 0.6) for intelligence, using IQ tests. (Newman et al, 1928; Shields, 1962.)

Some psychologists have used such results to argue that intelligence is, therefore, largely genetic. Hans Eysenck, for one, has notoriously claimed that about 80% of the variability is inborn.

Others argue that Twin Studies are not reliable or valid, for instance, because of small sample sizes or because some separated twins were raised in similar environments. For example, Kamin (1974) pointed out that at least one of Newman's "separated pairs" ended up in the same town and another in the same school!

Similar criticisms can be applied to twin research on schizophrenia. Some psychologists are not impressed...
So what? We still can't change what is inborn. So we need to concentrate on improving the environment!

The environment is the focus of the last perspective...

6. THE SOCIAL AND CULTURAL PERSPECTIVE

Behaviour is influenced by the environment in the broadest sense – through the family, social class, caste, tribe, religion, country, and culture in general. People are so familiar with their own upbringing and way of life that they often forget just how different it can be – not just in other countries but even next door!

This approach in psychology borrows or adapts many of its concepts from sociology and anthropology. For example, "socialization" – the process of learning the "norms" or rules of society.

The Comparative approach can also be useful...

This makes us aware of the DIFFERENCES and SIMILARITIES between us and others...

What Is Culture?

The problem is defining what culture is. We could call it the "human-made part of the environment" and say that it comes in two parts: **objective** (means of transport, cooking equipment, technology) and **subjective** (beliefs, values, roles).

The trouble is, culture isn't static but always changing.
So, there are "traditional" (slower to change) cultures and "modern" (faster to change) cultures...
Beware of thinking that "modern" is better because it "progresses" – to *what*?

"Culture" often refers to groups of countries – for instance, "Western", meaning the USA and most European nations. But this can miss out other relevant countries (Australia, Hong Kong, Japan) and differences within the grouping itself.

Cultural Analysis

Hofstede and Triandis have analyzed the differences between cultures.

Hofstede (1980): 4 Cultural Dimensions

1. Power Distance

– the respect and deference shown according to status

2. Uncertainty Avoidance

– the emphasis put on planning and stability

3. Individualism vs. Collectivism

– whether one's identity is personal, or from the group

e.g. The West = more Individualism; The East = more Collectivism

4. Masculinity vs. Femininity

– whether it's important to achieve goals ("masculine") or interpersonal harmony ("feminine")

e.g. Japan = Masculine; Sweden = Feminine

Triandis (1990): 3 major "Cultural Syndromes"

1. Cultural Complexity

e.g. the extent to which TIME or RELIGION is important

2. Individualism vs. Collectivism (similar to Hofstede's)

3. Tight vs. Loose

– whether one sticks to the norms, or is allowed to deviate

e.g. Japan = Tight; Thailand, Hong Kong, Singapore = Loose

Why are there so many different cultures? This fact leads to another problem...

Ethnocentrism

The tendency to use our own ethnic or cultural group's norms and values to define what's "natural" and "correct" is called "ethnocentrism". The dangers of extreme ethnocentrism should be well known lessons of history – especially where Nationalism has led to hatred and persecution. Sadly, such lessons still haven't been learned, even as we enter the 21st century.

Academic ethnocentrism is a problem in many subjects.

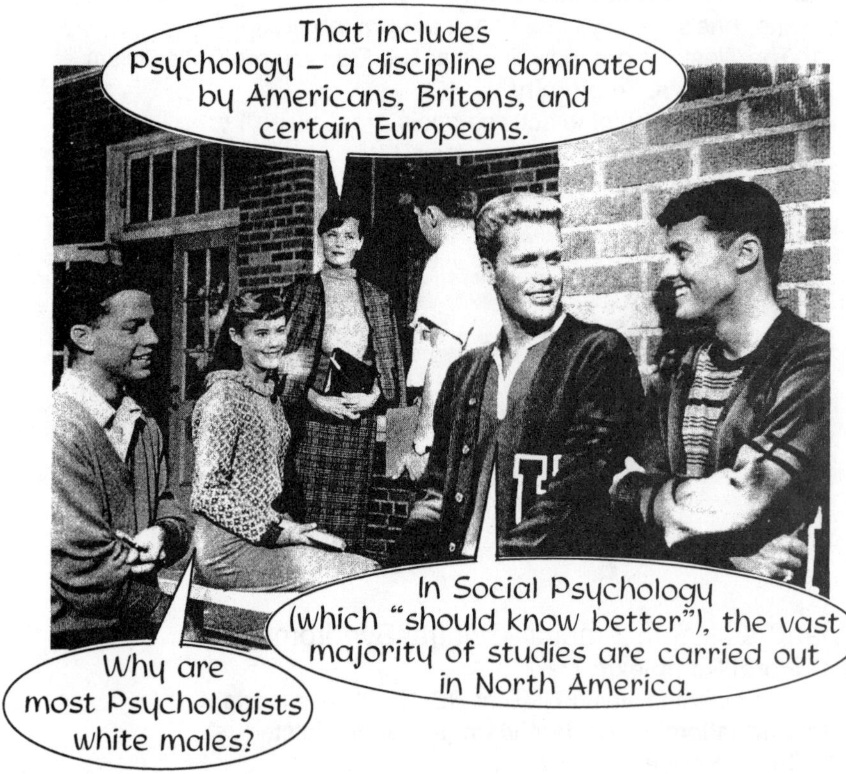

To further narrow the field, most participants in psychological research are university undergraduates in their late teens and early twenties!

The process of ethnocentrism is similar to racism and sexism – indeed any such prejudice.

One particularly famous cross-cultural study, however, was by a white female...

Cross-Cultural Research

Margaret Mead (1901-78) in *Sex and Temperament in Three Primitive Societies* (1935) described 3 tribes in New Guinea:
The Arapesh were mainly non-aggressive, males and females, with a warm, caring approach towards children.
The Mundugumor were aggressive, males and females, and were cold and uncaring towards children.
The Tchambuli were the most unusual since the males were submissive and passive.

We spend much of our time gossiping and putting on make-up.
While we females are dominant, aggressive and generally in control.
Children are encouraged to follow these roles.

The Tchambuli gender "role-reversal" (as Mead then saw it) is often quoted as evidence for "cultural relativism", against the "nature argument" that gender roles are the consequences of inborn sex differences.

Mead has been criticized for her subjective "participant observation" method of living with the tribes and recording certain behaviour. We also don't know about other possible influences, e.g. genetic or dietary. Anyway, these tribes represent only a tiny proportion of the world's population. Still, it does demonstrate that cultural relativism can be important, and not just for gender.

This concludes the six theoretical perspectives. In practice, the subject matter of Psychology is usually sectioned into four: Developmental, Social, Comparative and Individual Differences, as follows...

DEVELOPMENTAL PSYCHOLOGY

The Developmental section covers changes in behaviour from birth, so it's mainly about children. However, since development occurs throughout the whole of life, it also includes adolescence, adulthood and senescence (old age). Two particularly important Developmental Psychologists are Piaget and Bowlby.

Jean Piaget (1896-1980), studied cognitive development and showed that children are not just immature humans but people who *think differently* to adults. Piaget produced four inter-related theories.

1. STAGE THEORY: there are four stages of cognitive development.

(a) Sensorimotor Stage (0-2): the child learns about, and starts to control, its environment through the senses and motor (movement) abilities. Repetition is important...

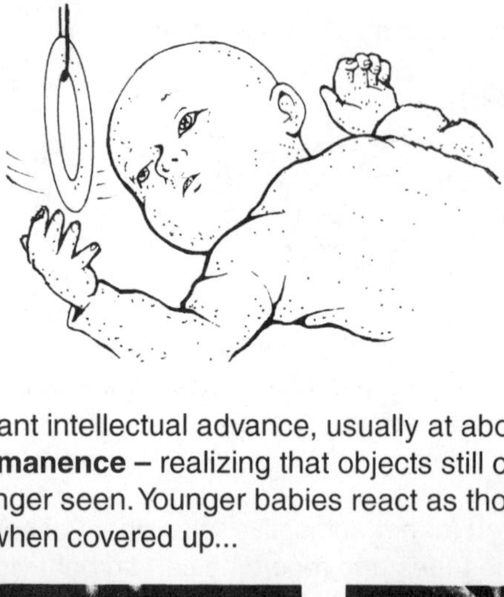

One important intellectual advance, usually at about 8 months, is **Object Permanence** – realizing that objects still continue to exist, even when no longer seen. Younger babies react as though objects disappear when covered up...

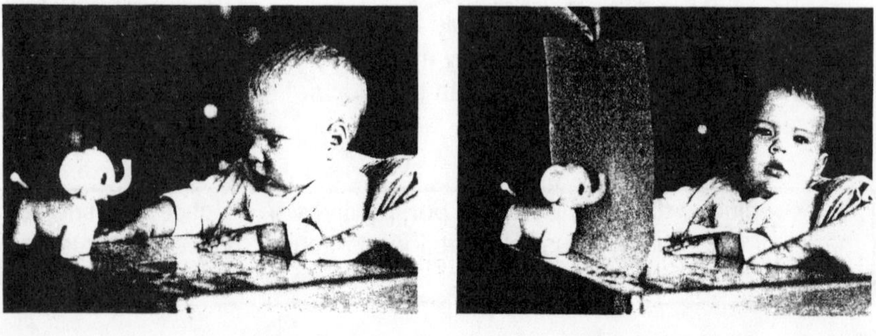

(b) Pre-Operational Stage (2-7): before the stage of real intellectual advance (which comes next), the child acquires language and eventually understands that other people see things differently.

At this stage, the young child is still "egocentric" and can't see from another's point of view.
But you MUST be able to see the house – I can!

(c) Concrete Operational Stage (7-11): when mental tasks (operations) can be performed, so long as objects are visible (concrete).

Conservation of Number Experiment

Two identical rows are seen. One is re-arranged in front of the child.

Now which row has most?
That one!

Result: children under 6 years cannot "Conserve Number" – they do not realize the number is the same even if the arrangement is different. From about 6 years they can Conserve Number, realizing that the arrangement is not relevant. Understanding about volume comes later.

(c) Concrete Operational Stage (continued)

Conservation of Mass Experiment

1. Young child looking at two ball-shaped pieces, same size
2. Adult makes one into a sausage-shape
3. Adult asks,

Now which one is the biggest?
That one!

Conservation of Volume Experiment

1. Young child looking at glasses, one tall-thin and one short-fat
2. Adult pours liquid from short-fat glass to tall thin one
3. Adult asks,

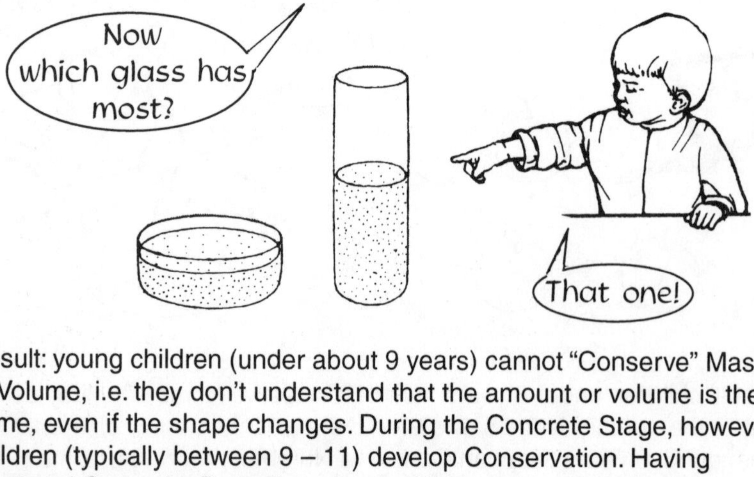

Now which glass has most?
That one!

Result: young children (under about 9 years) cannot "Conserve" Mass or Volume, i.e. they don't understand that the amount or volume is the same, even if the shape changes. During the Concrete Stage, however, children (typically between 9 – 11) develop Conservation. Having mastered Concrete Operations, each child moves to the last stage.

(d) Formal Operational Stage (11+): when mental tasks can be performed using abstract ideas – those that are not seen (not concrete).

Pendulum Experiment

What is most important for making the pendulum swing fast or slow?
(i) the size of weight?...
(ii) the length of string?...
(iii) how hard it's pushed?

Result: Children from about the age of 12 years can work this out. Answer: (ii) the length of string. (Not all adults reach this stage!)

Overall: The ages given are a rough guide. The main point is the *sequence* of stages. Even so, critics argue that Piaget was very pessimistic – children can perform tasks much younger, if problems are presented more interestingly. For example, McGarrigle and Donaldson, 1974, used a "Naughty Teddy Bear" who re-arranged things. The Stage Theory is relatively straightforward, but the next is less easy to understand.

2. SCHEMA THEORY explains how people, at all ages, develop concepts by building simple ideas into complex ones. A **schema** is a sort of fluid building-block or "mental action".

A neonate (new-born) has only a limited supply of simple schemas, e.g. the sucking reflex...
From this, by developing the use of the mouth, adding sounds, and acquiring language, eventually the highly complex schemas of speech appear!

Schemas (or schemata) develop through two processes:

(a) Assimilation (from biology) means "to take in", e.g. the early "Grasping Schema" enables the baby to grab and pick up small convenient objects.

(b) Accommodation (also from biology) means "to change", e.g. the "Grasping Schema" develops by altering to cater for objects different in size, shape and weight.

These two processes aren't only important to babies.

Adult Schemas

(a) Recognition is mainly Assimilation – taking in the surroundings, checking that things are the same, provides comfort and security.

(b) Learning, on the other hand, is mainly Accommodation – adding new information to *change* existing knowledge.

From the above examples, it follows that people need to experience both recognition (existing things) and learning (new things) on a daily basis. If there was too much recognition – if everything stayed the same – then life would be boring. If there was too much learning – i.e. constant newness – then life would be confusing.

Summary: The development and use of Schemas through Assimilation and Accommodation enables adaptation to the changing environment. ("Intelligence" is adapting quickly.) Adaptation is also a feature of the next theory.

3. PLAY THEORY

Piaget (1951) saw **PLAY** as an adaptive activity involving **mainly Assimilation**, whereby the child attempts to fit the world of reality into its own needs and experience...

IMITATION, on the other hand, is mainly **Accommodation** – the child changes its own behaviour by copying someone else.

Piaget emphasized that play is done for its own sake. The child "repeats his behaviour not in any further effort to learn or investigate but for the mere joy of mastering it" (Piaget, 1951).

There are 3 stages of play, corresponding to the first 3 stages of Cognitive Development...

(a) Mastery Play or Practice Play, since it is repetition of behaviour.

(b) Symbolic Play or Make-Believe Play, since it involves fantasy, role-playing and use of symbols.

Language itself is, of course, symbolism – a crucial aspect of this stage.

(c) Play With Rules, as it suggests, is when the child uses rules in games – which can sometimes dominate the play...

This ability to use rules is important in learning right from wrong...

4. MORAL THEORY

Piaget found that children under 9 typically decide what is "good" by using rules taught by others. In Piaget's terms, they are **heteronomous** (Greek, "from another"). Later, when they can decide more for themselves, they become **autonomous** ("from oneself"). Young children usually decide from the OUTCOME of actions, rather than the INTENTION. Piaget tested this by telling pairs of stories to each child...

"Child 1 deliberately spills a *little* milk on the carpet, whereas Child 2 accidentally spills a *lot* of milk on the carpet. Which one is naughtier?"

Piaget's Theories had a big impact, especially in Europe, on education. For example, since children develop at their own rates, many key cognitive abilities (e.g. Conservation of Number) cannot actually be taught. Therefore, teachers need to provide stimulating environments and encourage development through **Discovery Learning**.

Bowlby

John Bowlby (1907-90) concentrated on emotional development. He became famous after the World Health Organization (WHO) published a Monograph, *Maternal Care and Mental Health,* in 1951.

"Mother love is as important for development as vitamins and minerals..."

He found evidence that maternal deprivation correlates positively with juvenile delinquency (Bowlby, 1944), and so produced his (emotive!) conclusion that mothers should stay at home with their children.

This argument was used by governments to persuade mothers not to go out to work – a convenient ploy to get unemployed ex-servicemen back to work in the early 1950s.

Bowlby's other controversial belief was that children only form ONE strong emotional attachment, usually with the mother, called **Monotropy**.

Research on attachment has subsequently tended to be basically FOR or AGAINST Bowlby...

"For Bowlby"

(1) American Psychiatrists, especially H. M. Skeels and R. A. Spitz, found that babies in orphanages who were deprived of love and affection became emotionally withdrawn and "apathetic".

(2) Harry Harlow (1959) found that baby rhesus monkeys become attached to artificial "mothers" that have soft cloth bodies but supply no milk, rather than wire bodies that do.

Thus "Cupboard Love" is not the cause of attachment.

Furthermore, monkeys deprived of natural mothers grew up to be anti-social, have sexual problems, and be poor parents (Harlow, 1962).

"Against Bowlby"

(1) Anna Freud and Sophie Dann published a case study (1951) about a group of 6 orphans, all around three years old, rescued from a World War II concentration camp. They were brought to England and ended up at the Bulldog's Bank refugee centre, where they were extremely aggressive.

However, they apparently survived their psychological traumas, by bonding with each other, and became socially normal within about three years.

The long-term effects, though, are unclear.

(2) Cross-cultural studies have found that children often naturally bond with several people. For example, Mary Ainsworth (1967) studied the Ganda tribe of Uganda and found multiple attachments.

Both studies go against Bowlby's "Monotropy" theory.

Evaluation of Bowlby

Michael Rutter suggests Bowlby is partly right, partly wrong. Rutter's research on the Isle of Wight (Rutter, 1972) found significant positive correlations between family disruption and juvenile delinquency – supporting Bowlby. However, Bowlby's concept of maternal separation is too vague. Rutter usefully suggests distinguishing **deprivation**, i.e. *loss* or removal of a mother, from **privation**, i.e. *lack* of maternal care. Rutter also believes that other factors are important, e.g. it's *stress* rather than divorce itself that can be damaging.

Mavis Hetherington *et al* (1978) also found that stress created by parents, during divorce, can affect the children – causing anger, depression, and guilt.

Bowlby, therefore, was right to emphasize the importance of love and affection in childhood, and to warn about the link between lack of affection, and later delinquency.
However, it's not *only* the mother who is important, and whether the mother goes out to work or not is itself of little relevance.

Other influences come from a wide range of **social** factors.

SOCIAL PSYCHOLOGY

Social Psychology includes the study of:
Interpersonal Relationships (e.g. Perception of others, Attraction)
Personality (e.g. Types, Self-Concept, Attitudes)
Group Behaviour (e.g. Conformity, Obedience)

INTERPERSONAL RELATIONSHIPS, of course, can depend on the key *developmental* relationships formed in childhood and adolescence. Research mentioned here concentrates on the **perception of others** and **sexual attraction**.

(1) Perception of others is often based on key characteristics we think people have. Asch (1946) and Kelley (1950) found that we look for "Central Traits" (as opposed to "Peripheral Traits"), for example, a "warm" person who is generous, humorous, sociable; or the opposite, a "cold" person.

The **Halo Effect** occurs when we generalize a person's Central Traits.

For example, if someone is perceived as basically "good" or "likeable", then we tend to interpret *all* their behaviour as such.
They can do no wrong!

Similarly, someone perceived to be "bad" will tend to be disliked *whatever* they do!

The Primacy / Recency Effect refers to whether we discover information about someone earlier (Primacy) or later (Recency). The Primacy Effect – “first impressions count” – occurs from the moment of meeting a person (within seconds), and the effect of the face, clothes, mannerisms, speech..

Luchins (1957) found that people judged a person to be basically “introvert” or “extrovert” depending on the information given first, even when it was later contradicted.

(2) Sexual attraction

There are several processes that influence whether we like or love someone.

(a) **Compatibility**: people tend to "pair off" with those who are generally similar or "matching". This applies to physical attractiveness (Murstein, 1972) and other factors, such as education, IQ (Hatfield et al, 1978). Culture, especially religion, can also be important (Newcomb, 1961). Sometimes, though, it's a case of "opposites attract" (Winch 1955).

(b) **Rewards and Costs**: attention, affection, trust, security, sharing, skills, information, status, money, energy, reproduction, sex...
Some Psychologists (e.g. Blau, 1964; Homans, 1974; Berscheid and Walster, 1978) see relationships as being like an accountant's balance sheet:

Profit = Reward - Cost

There may also be a sense of **investment** in a relationship, and **compromises** based on **expectations**, e.g. "I don't expect a good-looking, rich wife/husband".

(c) **Specific Factors**

– Physical Attraction is initially important, especially for men (Walster et al, 1966)
– Familiarity and Exposure seems to increase liking (Festinger et al 1950; Zajonc et al 1971, 1974). (As used in advertising and political campaigning!)
– Reciprocal Liking – we tend to like people who we think like us! (Aronson, 1976)

Attitudes

This is Social Psychology's cornerstone. There's much research especially on changing attitudes for social control (war propaganda, political campaigning, health and safety) and advertising.

An attitude can be divided into 3 aspects:

1. **Cognitive** – the beliefs (factual & neutral) e.g."Smoking is a major cause of cancer".
2. **Affective** – the emotional feelings e.g. "I hate the smell of cigarettes".
3. **Behavioural** – the actions taken e.g. "I only eat in non-smoking restaurants".

Attitude change can be achieved by working on all three, especially the Affective component (Janis & Feshbach, 1953).

Data on attitudes is often collected by surveys, using "questionnaires" based on the designs of Thurstone (1929) and Likert (1932).

Attitude Questionnaire on Smoking

Please tick one box for each statement:

	Strongly Agree	Agree	Don't Know	Disagree	Strongly Disagree
Smoking is a major cause of cancer					
I hate the smell of cigarettes					
I only eat in non-smoking restaurants					

Prejudice can be seen as an extreme attitude that can be a useful learned response to avoid potential danger. (If certain food makes you ill, you'll avoid similar food). Or it can lead to irrational and antisocial behaviour, such as racism (Benson et al, 1976), sexism, ageism, speciesism.

Prejudice can be easily created, for instance, by saying that brown-eyed people are better than blue-eyed – as demonstrated by Jane Elliott (1977).

Prejudice reduction can be achieved by (i) non-competitive contact of an equal status, and (ii) pursuing common goals through co-operation (Brown, 1986).

Group Behaviour

Distinctions can be made between **Conformity** (influence of a group) and **Obedience** (instructions from a person).

Conformity

Asch (1951) found that a small group of people can influence a person to agree with an incorrect statement with about 1/3 always agreeing, and about 3/4 at least once. (Only 3 other people were required for maximum influence.) Reasons included...

This highlights the "sheep-like" nature of many people – very useful for socially acceptable behaviour (obeying the law, being polite, etc.); sometimes unfortunate (e.g. "fashion victims"); and potentially dangerous, as we'll see next.

Obedience

Milgram (1963) asked participants to act as "teacher" in a "learning" situation, giving increasingly larger "electric shocks" for each wrong answer. The "pupil" in the next room could be heard screaming, "I can't stand the pain!" (at "180 volts") and in agony (at "270 volts").

Despite protests, Milgram asked each participant to continue to a potentially lethal "450 volts".

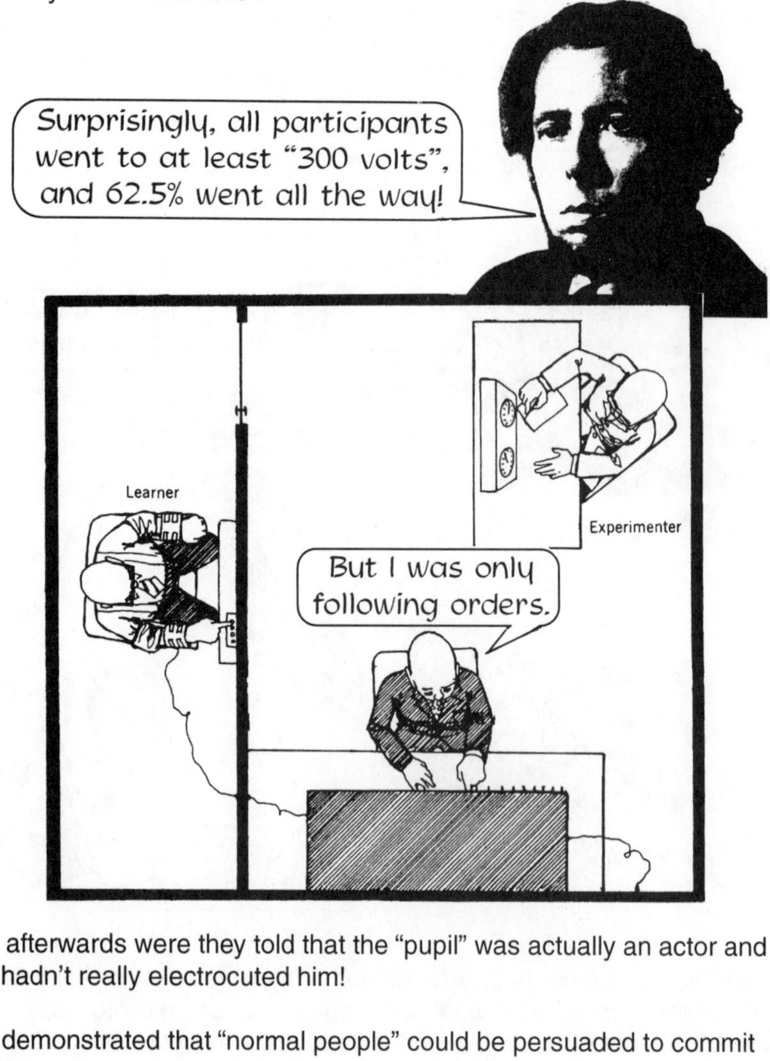

Only afterwards were they told that the "pupil" was actually an actor and they hadn't really electrocuted him!

This demonstrated that "normal people" could be persuaded to commit crimes.

COMPARATIVE PSYCHOLOGY

Animals are studied in order to **compare** them to humans, but they are also interesting in their own right.

This section of psychology is sometimes crudely divided into "laboratory" and "natural" research – the latter being strongly influenced by **ethologists**, like Lorenz and Tinbergen who studied animals in their natural habitats.

The "laboratory" studies have provided the four main theories of learning that we have already covered in the Behaviourism and Cognitive Perspectives.

Summary of Learning Theories:

1. Classical Conditioning (Pavlov) – p.61
2. Operant Conditioning (Skinner) – p.76
3. Social Learning (Bandura) – p.88
4. Cognitive Learning (Köhler) – p.98

The "natural" studies have provided a lot of insights into social behaviour, especially communication and aggression.

Animal Societies

Why do many animals form social groups? In one word: SURVIVAL! This applies to both INDIVIDUAL and SPECIES survival.

Individual Survival requires **protection** (including shelter from the weather and getting **food**).

Species Survival requires **reproduction** (involving finding a suitable mate, courtship and bonding, and **protecting others** (especially the off-spring).

Of course, most of these are inborn, automatic INSTINCTS involving little conscious decision-making. In fact, we have to beware of putting human interpretations on animal behaviour, i.e. we should avoid **anthropomorphism** ("human likeness")...

Communication

In order for these survival processes to work, there has to be some form of **communication**. Usually this takes the form of SIGNS that can be visual, auditory or olfactory – for example, a pheromone (= smelly hormone). A male moth can smell a female half a mile away!

Some signs are fairly universal but some are unique to the species.

But however complex the communication is, whether it's bird-song, whale-song, dolphin clicks or monkey calls, there hasn't yet been discovered any real **syntax** or **grammar**. It is therefore generally believed that there is no true "language" apart from that of humans. Possible exceptions include research on chimps using American Sign Language (as used by deaf people), e.g. "Washoe" taught by Gardner and Gardner (1971, '75, '78, '83). However, some critics suggest that such communication, however impressive, is still mainly imitation (Terrace, 1979).

Aggression

Even though most animals have only simple forms of communication, compared to the complexity of human languages, they often seem to be much better at avoiding serious injury or death to those of the same species! **Social Facilitation** is behaviour that's pro-social rather than anti-social – e.g. yawning, scratching, not staring.

When conflicts do arise, when competing for a mate or defending territory, animals will typically use **Ritualized Aggression**.

One makes threatening noises and postures.
While the other submits and retreats, thus avoiding a fight.

Even if physical contact does occur, it's usually in such a way that serious injury is unlikely, for instance, by using tough parts of the body, as with two goats banging their heads together.

Actually, murder, i.e. intentional killing of a member of the same species, is rare. Jane Goodall studied chimps in the wild for over twelve years before witnessing the first murder!

INDIVIDUAL DIFFERENCES

This considers **normality and abnormality,** with the emphasis on **psychological health** and **illness (diagnosis** and **therapy).** Two specific areas are: **intelligence** and **personality.**

What is "normal"?

Richard Gross (1996) suggests several meanings:
1. A Statistical Definition (value-free): whatever the vast majority do (95%) is normal; the minority (5%) is abnormal. (Statistically: anything more than 2 Standard Deviations from the Mean.)

2. Deviation-from-the-Norm (value-judgements): what's socially acceptable. For example, in some cultures homosexuality is "unnatural", "sinful", "unhealthy", "sick", "perverse", "revolting", "a threat to civilization", etc. But other cultures do not make this value-judgement.

3. Mental Health attempts to define a mature, fulfilled human being. This includes being aware of what we're doing and why; personal development; ability to cope with stress; independence; conceiving reality; ability to love and be loved; having satisfactory personal relationships. (Jahoda, 1958.)

4. Mental Illness includes 2 subjective views: (a) "Others think I'm OK, but I'm distressed." (b) "I'm OK – others think otherwise!" Mostly, these are attempts at objective criteria, usually based on a medical model – or a rejection of it.

Anti-psychiatrist R. D. Laing (1959,1961)

Psychopathology

"Pathological" means "diseased", so literally this is about "mental illness". But today the term "**mental disorder**" is preferred. In practice, there are two main classification systems:

1. **The ICD** – International Classification of Diseases – issued by the World Health Organization (WHO). The tenth version, ICD-10 (1987), is used in Britain and elsewhere.
2. **The DSM** – Diagnostic and Statistical Manual (of Mental Disorders) – issued by The American Psychiatric Association. The fourth edition, DSM-IV (1993), is used in the USA and elsewhere.

These are very similar. Both derive from Emil Kraepelin's (1896) classification. In addition to "organic" disorders, with biological causes, a distinction has traditionally been made between "neurosis" and "psychosis".

Neurotic
– only part of personality affected
– person is aware
e.g. phobias, obsessions, anxiety

Psychotic
– whole personality affected
– person is not aware
e.g. schizophrenia

There are also **Mood** ("affective") disorders – e.g. depression, mania – and **Personality** disorders, e.g. anti-social behaviour ("psychopathy"), dependency.

Therapy can be based on any of the six Perspectives. Attempts at finding "which one is best?" show that about 2/3 of patients can benefit from therapies, but about 2/3 improve ("spontaneous remission") without ANY treatment! (Eysenck, 1952). The question, though, is unhelpful. The type of therapy needed depends a lot on the problem – just as medicine does.

Today, therapy is often **eclectic**, based on a combination of drugs and a mixture of Psychological techniques.

IQ Tests

The first tests were created by **Alfred Binet** (1905) for use by French schools to identify and help less able school children. These tests produced a simple number, or **quotient**, summarizing abilities.

An IQ of 100 was chosen as the convenient average and the Normal Curve describes the distribution of scores (1 Standard Deviation is usually about 15 IQ points)...

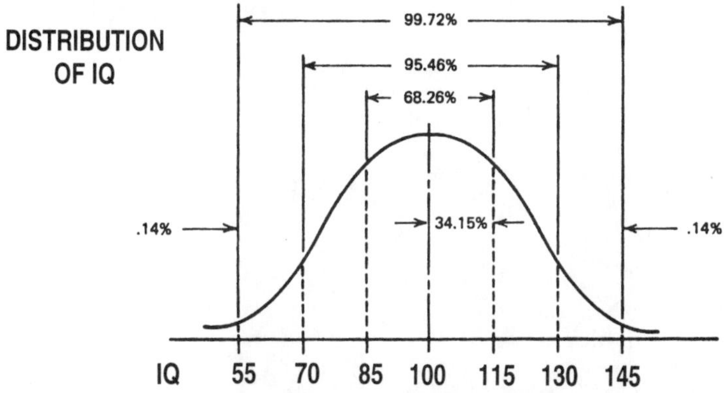

IQ tests were developed at Stanford University (USA) – "Stanford-Binet" tests – from 1916. Governments used them for armed services recruitment.

Today, various IQ tests are used in schools, for job recruitment, personal development, etc. These include the Wechsler and Eysenck tests.

Example IQ question: 3 8 12 15 17 ?

IQ Controversies

Intelligence is probably the most controversial topic in Psychology! This is partly due to the use of IQ tests as selection tools – especially in schools. Instead of, for example, using them to help children (as Binet intended), the British only helped some.

Even more controversially, IQ tests have been quoted for racial differences. For instance, Arthur Jensen (1969) concluded that blacks "test about fifteen IQ points below the average of the white population". Hans Eysenck (1981) affirmed, "These results are culture-fair... We conclude that a simple model giving a heritability of something like 80% for IQ is both realistic and defensible".

Certain psychologists have given IQ tests, and themselves, a "bad name". Although, to be fair to Eysenck, he did emphasize:

"The error is to exaggerate the importance of intelligence. The facts and arguments can easily be abused by racists... Each person has to be treated as an individual."

Most importantly, research shows that improving the environment *can* significantly improve IQ (Skeels, 1966). IQ tests have, anyway, been criticized for not being VALID: testing only certain abilities and not being representative of others – e.g. not including "practical sense" or solving everyday challenges.

The problem here is definition. A circular argument has been created – "Intelligence is what IQ tests measure". Others (Piaget) have tried to break out of this, but IQ tests remain a dominant tool.

(Answer to IQ question on page 161 = 18)

Personality

"Personality" (Latin "persona", actor's mask) is also hard to define – and another focus for the Nature-Nurture debate.

Type Theories
Some Psychologists have concentrated on general personality "**Types**". For example, C. G. Jung's **Introvert** or **Extravert** developed by Hans Eysenck using his questionnaires (EPI, EPQ) along with a **Neurotic – Stable** dimension. Eysenck argued that these are mainly inborn.

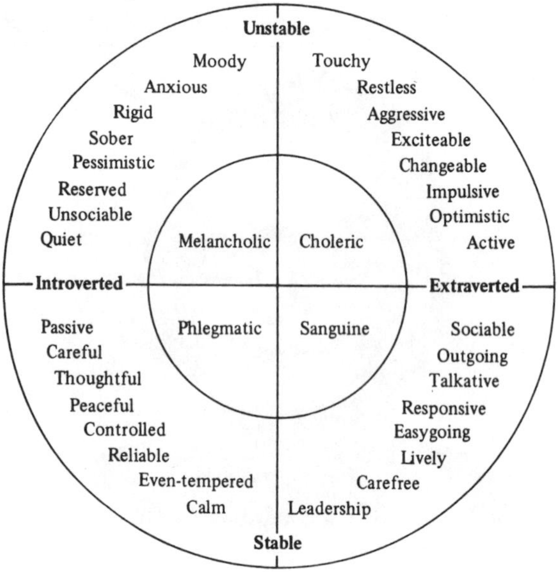

Another popular "type" theory is by Friedman and Rosenman (1959). Type A people are competitive, impatient, restless and prone to heart-disease, cancer, etc. Type B personalities are not.

Trait Theories
Others have identified characteristics or "**Traits**", e.g. Cattell's 16 Personality Factors (measured by his "16PF" questionnaire), including: submissive-dominant, trusting-suspicious, practical-imaginative...

Such questionnaires are the basis of **psychometrics**, which measures personality quantitatively. They're not available to the public and should only be used by qualified people. (Although misuse is common, especially among employers.)

PSYCHOLOGY TODAY

Psychologists today generally use all Perspectives, although a few still are entrenched, narrow-minded and dismissive of other views. Similarly, few still argue about the Nature-Nurture Debate, since both are important and can't be separated – the "Interactionist" view.

There are also now other important viewpoints.

Feminism and Racism

Since the 1970s, there's been much more awareness of the inequalities that can exist in society generally. Psychology, like most subjects, is still embarrassingly short of key female and non-white teachers, researchers and writers.

Psychology still tends to present human behaviour using heterosexual white-males as the norm against which all else is compared.
This isn't only a matter of personal injustice to those who could make valuable contributions, given more opportunities, but a case of possibly massive "white masculine bias" in the subject as a whole.

Feminists have identified and highlighted these problems and, furthermore, made us aware of other biases and injustices – prejudice against disabilities, old age, sexual preferences, animals ("speciesism").

Ethics of Human Research

Surprisingly, it's only been relatively recently that concerns about the ethics of research have strongly influenced psychologists. Further impetus for this came in the wake of certain American studies (e.g. Milgram's experiments) which deliberately put people under tremendous stress.

Codes of Conduct and **Ethical Principles** have been published by the APA (1953, 1983) and the BPS (1978, 1985, 1990) which must be followed by Psychologists in all research, practice and teaching.

Main Ethical Concepts

Voluntary Participation is important, including the right to withdraw at any stage.
Informed Consent should be obtained from participants, including permission to publish results.
Deception should be avoided or, if essential at first, participants should be informed as soon as possible.
De-briefing (and, if necessary, counselling) should be provided.
Confidentiality should be maintained, including anonymity in publication, to prevent tracing of participants.
Physical and Mental Harm should be avoided, including embarrassment, humiliation, damage to self-esteem.
Professional Conduct by the Psychologist(s), including integrity, responsibility, accountability, monitoring of other researchers, etc.

What about us?

Ethics of Animal Research

The reasons for animal research:
(a) There are sufficient similarities to make comparisons with humans.
(b) Similar human research would not be practical or ethical.

This can create "The Animal Research Paradox": if animals are similar enough to compare, then they may be similar enough to suffer as well!

In the past, some animal experiments have undoubtedly caused physical and mental suffering.
Many would not be allowed today because of the legal requirements.

In Britain, there is the *Animals Scientific Procedures Act* (1986) and other professional codes (e.g. the BPS *Guidelines for the Use of Animals in Research*, 1985). The "Animals Act" of 1986 requires Home Office licenses for premises, individuals and each project, with strict regulations.

The BPS "Guidelines" oblige researchers to follow a checklist, including:
– *Avoid, or at least minimize, discomfort*
– *Discuss... with Home Office Inspector and colleagues*
– *Seek... widespread advice as to whether the likely scientific contribution... justifies the use of living animals, and whether the scientific point they wish to make may not be made without the use of living animals.*

In practice today, "the use of animals for psychological research represents a tiny fraction of the use of animals for research in general" (Gross, 1996).

Brief Guide to Further Issues and Applications

1. Psychology as an Academic Subject

Psychology as an academic subject is usually divided into various departmental sections representing specialisms for teaching, exam and research purposes. These departments typically include the four sections outlined – Developmental, Social, Comparative and Individual Psychology – plus Cognitive and Bio-Psychology.

There can be overlaps between the sections, but Psychodynamic, Behaviourist and Humanistic perspectives do not tend to have corresponding departments. The Psychodynamic is often based in the Developmental or Individual Differences Section. Behaviourism may be included in both of these as well, but it's often mainly in Comparative Psychology. The Humanistic approach is often dealt with in Individual Differences.

Usually, university departments consist of Psychologists from several backgrounds. For instance, a Cognitive Dept. may include specialists in Bio-Psychology, Developmental, Individual, and Cognitive Psychology.

2. Current Trends

Two particularly strong sections are Cognitive and Health Psychology.

Cognitive Psychology (or "**Cognitive Science**", as many prefer) is seen as providing solutions to numerous problems by applying its research on (appropriately!) problem-solving, and pursuing the complexities of thinking. It benefits greatly from computers for directly testing participants and general analysis.

Health Psychology is a relatively new application of all perspectives and other sections, especially Individual Differences. Personality theories, Psychopathology and Psychotherapy (any recognized therapies) can be applied to coping with stress, bereavement, marriage and divorce, self-destructive behaviour (smoking, alcoholism), sexual behaviour, etc. Health Psychology can help people understand that much of their fate is in their own hands and habits. A related popular application is **Sports Psychology**, which includes motivation, self-concept, group dynamics, etc.

Both these applications are benefitting from the advances in biology, e.g. the Human Genome Project.

3. The Demand for Psychology

There is a *rapidly* growing demand for Psychology. Books, and other media versions, sell well – even though it's mainly at the "Popular Psychology" end of the market (an unfortunate term, increasingly used in bookshops). Sadly, of course, this is polluted by the dross of charlatans out to make easy money! Usually, biographical notes and quality reviews give some guide to value.

College and university courses in Psychology, and courses featuring it as a secondary subject, are becoming ever more popular. In Britain, it's the second most popular degree course next to Law. In the USA, Psychology is also the second largest Major after Business Administration & Management.

4. The Status of Psychology

One major concern is the fact that virtually anyone can legally call themselves a "psychologist", regardless of qualifications and experience. Particularly worrying is that people set themselves up as "therapists" or even "psychotherapists" (which can be a misleading or even meaningless title) and attempt to treat people.

In Britain, the BPS has created a voluntary "Register of Chartered Psychologists" (1990) of qualified members who provide services and the public can check this. But it hasn't yet achieved legal status. The Government needs to enforce a system similar to medical doctors. Professional associations (BPS, APA, APS, etc.) need to do much more in order to organize the profession and present a positive image of Psychology.

5. The Need for Psychology

In recent years, in most modern societies, there's been an increase in psychological problems – especially depression and stress-induced illnesses.

General Needs

Along with high standards of living, many people have high expectations (both for themselves and others) and are easily frustrated, impatient, and disappointed – with subsequent feelings of depression. Psychology can continue identifying such social problems, and offer ways for tackling them at both individual and institutional levels. Sadly, many still don't know what's available. Much more needs to be done to provide help and information, and encourage self-help.

State Education in many countries is seen to be failing children. Teachers and parents need to be trained to identify problems and use the various techniques available to help solve them. Teacher-training should include much more on intellectual development, learning theories and their application (including discipline), moral education, encouragement of independence, acceptance of responsibilities, building of self-esteem, etc.

Public Health services could provide a wider range of therapies. Traditional medicine still tends to give pills for symptoms, without considering the psychological picture. Relaxation and imaging techniques could be provided and taught to those with stress-related illnesses to facilitate recovery and prevent further illness. States of mind can seriously affect bodily functions, e.g. chronic stress debilitates the immune system. More research is needed.

Social Control is a third major application, in the areas of law enforcement, courts, punishment and rehabilitation. It *is* possible to change a lot of behaviour by using Behavioural techniques (Counter-conditioning, Aversion, Behaviour Modification, Modelling, etc.) plus Cognitive and Humanistic approaches (e.g. Problem-solving education and Self-Concept management).

A major problem with most penal systems is that they are unscientific. Assumptions are made about what will change behaviour, without proper testing and monitoring. Even when "punishment" doesn't work (as in the huge re-offending rates for ex-prisoners), there's little attempt to alter it. The judgements and convictions of courts are, anyway, usually based on a mish-mash of personal or legal opinion, public pressure, social isolation, revenge, and tradition – before any considerations of social rehabilitation.

Political Needs

The criticism that legal systems are often unscientific applies to politics in general. Huge assumptions are made about "what the people want" and "what is good for them", without much effort to get empirical evidence or test the theories. There's a case to be made for a new approach – "Psychopolitics" (to coin a phrase) – which benefits both from current psychological research and historical lessons.

In the wrong hands, of course, Psychopolitics could be dangerous. A democratically elected government could stay in power indefinitely if it was able to accurately assess public demand and satisfy that (at least long enough to get through the next election!).

On the positive side, though, a deeper understanding of human needs – together with a general scientific approach and empirical evidence – could help do away with the bad laws and time-wasting.

6. The Need for Philosophy

Psychology as a discipline could benefit from recombining with some of the philosophy that it was earlier so careful to distance itself from. As well as the "techniques" of philosophy (e.g. logical reasoning, identifying arguments and fallacies), Psychologists could learn much from the Big Issues – the definition of consciousness, the mind-body debate, the role of faith in thinking, free-will vs. determinism, and **ethics**.

Psychologists need to be trained to deal with the huge responsibilities and moral choices inherent in their work. Otherwise, they may seek to do good without realizing the harm that can be done. Philosophy can provide important insights into the very practical problems of morality.

7. Careers in Psychology

Having qualified as a Psychologist, a person can go into a wide range of professions – although it's often necessary to gain further qualifications, e.g. a Post-Graduate Diploma, Masters Degree or PhD.

CLINICAL PSYCHOLOGIST

EDUCATIONAL PSYCHOLOGIST **FORENSIC PSYCHOLOGIST** **PSYCHOLOGY LECTURER**

Further useful information is available from: The British Psychological Society, St. Andrew's House, 48 Princess Road East, Leicester, LE1 7DR

Psychology has a huge amount to offer for those who are willing to take the time and trouble to study it in some depth, and apply the findings to their lives and those around them. It's hoped that this book has provided a useful introduction and summary of the subject as a whole, encouraging further interest and application.

Acknowledgments

Mark Andrews – Artist, Graphic Designer
Pam Berry – Counsellor
Steve Brammell – Philosopher
Jenny Doe – Clinical Psychologist
Mike Gibas & John Read at 'Nomad', Letchworth – Graphic Designers
William Grieg – Layout Assistant, etc.
Linda Hambleton – Organizational Psychologist
Peter Kewley – Librarian, Researcher
Lorna Marriott – Paste-up Artist
Christine Pinkerton – Layout Assistant
John Radford – Distinguished Teacher (in the lecture hall and the pub!)
Eppie Saunders – Layout Assistant
Lee Stanley – Photographer

Bibliography, References and Further Reading

These are the main sources of information. Texts strongly recommended for further reading are in bold. [Square brackets show comments or p. numbers for quotations, references, etc. in this book.]

Angell, James R. (1904) *Psychology* Henry Holt and Co. New York pp 6-7, in Lundin, Robert (1996) p125 [p. 46 – quote]

Angell, James R. (1906) Presidential Address to the A.P.A. "The Province of Functional Psychology", in Lundin, Robert (1996) pp 125-6 [p. 46 – ref] NB The bubble on consciousness is not quoted from Angell but Schultz p.164.

Atkinson et al (1996) *Hilgard's Introduction to Psychology* (12th Ed.) Harcourt Brace. [Standard American undergraduate textbook.]

Baars (1986) p 275, in Schultz (1996) p 451 [p. 104 – quote (rat)]

Bandura *et al* (1963), in Gross (1996). [pp. 88-9 – ref]

Bowlby J. (1951) *Maternal care and mental health* WHO, Geneva. (p. 145)

Cardwell, Mike et al (1997) *Psychology* Collins Educational. [British textbook for Modular 'A' level.]

Colman, A. M. (1995) *Controversies in Psychology* Longman.

Coolican, Hugh et al (1996) *Applied Psychology*. Hodder & Stoughton. [Excellent summaries of key areas, e.g. Clinical, Criminological, Educational, Health, Occupational, Sport.]

Eysenck, Michael (1997) *Simply Psychology*. Collins.[British GCSE textbook.]

Fuller, Ray *et al* (1997) *A Century of Psychology* Routledge, London and New York. [Good collection of articles on the 20th century.]

Goleman (1983) p 54, in Schultz (1996) p 451. [p. 104 – quote]

Gross, Richard (1995) *Themes, Issues and Debates in Psychology.* Hodder & Stoughton.

Gross, Richard (1996) *Psychology – The Science of Mind and Behaviour* (3rd Ed.). Hodder & Stoughton. [British 'A' level text – excellent.]

Harlow, H. (1959) and (1962), in Gross (1996). [p. 146 – ref]

Hofstede (1980), in Gross (1996). [p. 133]

Hutt, C. (1972) *Males and Females.* Penguin, England. [p. 126 – ref]

Jones, Mary Cover (1924) in Schultz (1996) pp 272-3 [p. 75 – ref (not a true quote)]

Kamin, L. (1981) *Intelligence: The Battle For The Mind* (Eysenck vs Kamin). Pan. [p. 130 – ref]

Lewin, K. (1936) *Principles of Topological Psychology.* McGraw-Hill. [p. 103]

Lewin *et al* (1939) in Gross (1996). [p. 103]

Lundin, Robert W. (1996) *Theories and Systems of Psychology* (5th Ed.) Heath and Co. Lexington, USA. [Strong on theories and history.]

Maccoby, E. and Jacklin, C. (1974) *The Psychology of Sex Differences.* Stanford University Press, USA. [p. 126 – ref]

McIntyre, A. (1972) Sex differences in children's aggression. *Proceedings of 80th Annual Convention of APA.* 7:93-94

Marx, Karl and Engels, Frederick (1848, 1996) *The Communist Manifesto* Pluto Press, London. [Marx quoted from p 48 on p. 20.]

O'Donohue, William and Kitchener, Richard (1996) *The Philosophy of Psychology* Sage, London and California. [Good critical analysis of philosphical issues, e.g. ethics in chapter 25]

Pavlov, I. (1926) "Relation between Excitation and Inhibition... Experimental Neuroses in Dogs", in Pavlov (1955). p 235 [p. 63 – 2nd and 3rd quotes]

Pavlov, I. (1934) "The Conditioned Reflex", in Pavlov (1955). p 252 [p. 63 – 1st quote]

Pavlov, I. (1955) *Selected Works.* Foreign Languages Pub. House. Moscow.

Piaget (1932, '50, '63, '70, etc.) in Gross (1996). [pp. 36-41 – cognitive dev. ref; pp. 142-3 play ref; p. 144 – moral dev. ref]

Popper, K. (1968) *Conjecture and Refutations.* Harper Row, New York. [pp. 20-22 – ref]

Robinson, Daniel N. (1986) *An Intellectual History of Psychology* Univ. of Wisconsin Press. USA. [Good at linking Philosophy to Psychology.] [Watson quoted from p 405 on p. 72.]

Sacks, Oliver (1970) in (1990) *The Man Who Mistook His Wife for a Hat, and Other Clinical Tales.* Harper Perennial. New York. p 11 [p. 14 – quote]

Schultz, D. P. and Schultz, S. E. (1996) *A History of Modern Psychology* (6th Ed.) Harcourt Brace. USA [Excellent for history.]

Skinner, B. F. (1971) *Beyond Freedom and Dignity.* Pelican, England. p 20 [p. 4 – quote] (For Skinner, 1938 and 1953, see p. 76.)

Sternberg, R. J. (1995) *In Search of the Human Mind.* Harcourt Brace. [American undergraduate text.]

Sternberg, R. J. (1997) *Pathways to Psychology.* Harcourt Brace.

Triandis (1990) in Gross (1996). [p. 133]

Triplett, Norman (1898) The dynamogenic factors in pacemaking and competition. *American Journal of Psychology*, 9, 507-33 in Gross (2nd Edition, 1992) p 554: [p. 11 – ref]

Wade, Carole and Tavris, Carol (1990) *Psychology* (2nd Ed.) Harper & Row. [American undergraduate text.]

Watson, John B. (1913) *Psychology as the Behavorist Views It,* in Schultz (1996). pp 259-2 [p. 4 – quote; p. 72 – quote]

Watson, John B. (1930) *Behavorism.* (Rev. ed.) Norton, New York pp 303-4, in Schulltz (1996) pp 275-6 [p. 75 – quote]

Wellings, Kaye *et al* (1994) *Sexual Behaviour in Britain.* Penguin. UK and USA. [p.13 – ref and quote]

Wollheim, Richard (1971) *Freud.* Fontana Modern Masters, London. [Good summary of Freud's biography and theories.]

Wundt, Wilhelm (1873-4) *Principles of Physiological Psychology* (Preface), in Schultz (1996) p 72 [p. 25 – 1st quote]

Wundt, Wilhelm from Diamond (1980) A plea for historical accuracy. (Letter to the editor). *Contemporary Psychology*, 25, 84-5, in Schultz (1996) p 76 [p. 25 – 2nd quote]

Wundt, Wilhelm ("Rules of introspection") in Schultz (1996) p 78 [p. 25 – 3rd quote]

INDEX